"Courtship, dating, and marriage have become flashpoints of debate among young evangelicals – and this is a controversy worth our attention. Alex and Marni Chediak offer sound biblical advice and a clear Christian framework for working through the maze of confusions surrounding modern marriage. Against the stream of our postmodern culture committed to personal autonomy, this couple points Christians to a higher standard – the glory of God. Christians young and old, single and married, will find help in this concise book."

R. Albert Mohler, Jr., President
The Southern Baptist Theological Seminary,
Louisville, Kentucky

"If only courtship and marriage were so simple that all we needed was a manual to figure them out! The Chediaks give us something a better: a compass and a travel guide for the serious pilgrim. True north is the glory of God – get that straight and everything else will fall in place, miss it and nothing works. The rest is details, matters of topography and climate local customs. That too the Chediak's provide with warmth, wisdom and good humor of those who know the road and some of its potholes!"

Ben Patterson, College Pastor,
Westmont College, Santa Barbara, California

"Dating books are often read mainly by college students or single professionals. And that makes sense; it is natural for singles to seek wisdom on an issue they face daily. What makes *With One Voice* unique, however, is that it shows how a theology of marriage, and convictions regarding manhood and womanhood, are undeniably connected to how singles date and marry (or not). Rooted in a biblical worldview that keeps God central, *With One Voice* will be a helpful book for parents, married couples, and singles alike.

Rick Holland, Pastor of College and Student Ministries
Grace Community Church, Sun Valley, California

With One Voice

singleness, dating, and marriage
– to the glory of God

Alex Chediak & Marni Chediak

CHRISTIAN FOCUS

Copyright © Alex Chediak 2006

ISBN 1-85792-124-1

10 9 8 7 6 5 4 3 2 1

Published in 2006
by
Christian Focus Publications,
Geanies House, Fearn, Ross-shire,
IV20 1TW, Scotland

www.christianfocus.com

Cover design by Moose77 Designs

Printed and bound by
Nørhaven Paperback A/S

Contents

About the Authors

Alex & Marni Chediak seek to glorify God with one voice, sharing the life goal of being marked mainly as those who love God. As an expression of his desire to delight in the Lord, Alex has had the privilege of being involved in singles and college ministry, multi-generational small group ministry, as well as pulpit teaching and exposition. He is currently an apprentice at The Bethlehem Institute in Minneapolis, MN under the direction of Pastors John Piper and Tom Steller. He is also a professor at Northwestern College in Roseville, MN. Alex aspires to continue writing on culturally relevant topics from a God-centered perspective, and contributing to church-based adult Christian education. Alex was the general editor of _Five Paths to the Love of Your Life,_ published by NavPress in 2005. His wife Marni has had a career in management with Fortune 500 companies while ministering through Bible Study Fellowship and teaching Sunday school. She now enjoys using her many gifts assisting Alex in his callings. They are currently expecting their first child. Alex & Marni can be reached at With1Voice@gmail.com.

Preface

This book is about living to the glory of God in singleness and marriage. My assumption is that some of you reading this book are single and wondering how God might have you go about the process of marrying, or whether you even should marry. Others of you are probably married and have children or friends for whom you are praying. Still others are pastors in a position to give counsel to others.

The process of romance for unmarried Christians is about as complicated for singles today as it has ever been. Dangers lie everywhere. The world's perverse lies have infiltrated the church, reducing the beauty of God-invented sexuality to mere acts of personal pleasure. On the other hand, the increased geographic mobility, sheer number of possible work schedules, and career-based educational needs associated with modern life often make it more unlikely that singles will settle down in biblically based communities. In a day that values emotional fulfillment, many wonder if marriage is even necessary, given the commitment level and regular safeguarding and sacrifice it requires. Likewise, clear thinking on what it means to be a man and what it means to be a woman has been blurred by a worldview that has encouraged us to think of men and women as interchangeable and has called any discussion of innate differentiation "sexist".

This book is here to help. It does not contain a formula that guarantees relational happiness. It starts off showing how singleness in Western culture has changed, and why things are now so complicated. Chapter 2 discusses issues singles face associated with the question of "singleness versus marriage" and describes why lifelong marriage, though less common today, is still God's plan for most of us. We'll show that it is more important to *become* a certain type of person than it is to *find* a certain type of girlfriend/boyfriend. We'll see how holding up marriage as the purpose of dating or courting sets an appropriate tenor to the relationship. Chapters 3 and 4 delve into the thorny and often debated issues of manhood and womanhood. How does one's sense of masculinity and femininity affect how (and who) one goes about dating? Chapter 5 then gets into the nitty-gritty of wisely choosing a girlfriend/boyfriend that one can hopefully marry. Finally, chapter 6 will talk about the practicalities of the relationship process and how factors such as age and maturity should be considered.

I pray this book will be helpful for you, and that in your singleness and future marriage you would aim to glorify God above all else.

> "For a day in your courts is better than a thousand elsewhere. I would rather be a doorkeeper in the house of my God than dwell in the tents of wickedness. For the LORD God is a sun and shield; the LORD bestows favor and honor. No good thing does he withhold from those who walk uprightly" (Ps. 84:10-11).

Alex and Marni Chediak
October 2005, Eagan, MN, USA

1
Tracking the Changes

The Big Day

The big day had finally arrived – Sally and Tom were getting married at last! Sally had been looking forward to the day, planning it with her friends and mother. The flowers were just right, their hair and makeup looked beautiful, and the weather was turning out to be absolutely perfect. Sally, 28, has lived on her own in several different cities, so it was a bit of a chore for Sally to have to round up so many groups of friends from different eras of her life. Tom, 32, had a similar situation. He had his high school buddies from his home town of Raleigh, North Carolina, his college buddies from Syracuse, a crew from Long Island where he interned for a few years after college, and now his Boston, MA group where he and Sally met. He ended up with three groomsmen – one from college, another from Syracuse, and a third from Boston, with his best friend from high school as best man.

Sally's and Tom's families got along well. Sally had come over to Tom's home last Christmas. She enjoyed meeting Mr. and Mrs. Ratcliff, and Tom's sisters Veronica and Jessica. The five days went by fast, as they had to get to Sally's family in Florida for New Year. Mr. and Mrs. Schmitter enjoyed interacting with Tom. The two seemed to have a lot in common with their in-laws to be; both Tom and Mr. Schmitter were in the graphic arts industry. Sally was a research chemist, and Mr. Ratcliff did materials research and testing for Boeing.

At the festivities leading up to the wedding in Sally's hometown of Tallahassee, the Schmitters and the Ratcliffs were commenting on the differences between their children's wedding and their own. Bob and Gena Schmitter had married when Bob was 20 and Gena was 19. Bob worked his way through college on an Air Force ROTC plan, and there developed his interest in graphic arts. Gena worked as a receptionist and later as an office manager for two years before Bob graduated and they started having a family. Their fourth child had just left home for a specialty college program in California. Michael and Becky Ratcliff met in a small Christian college just outside Raleigh. After dating for three years, they married two weeks after graduating, and Michael began graduate studies in materials research while Becky worked as a product manager for a local firm. Twenty-five years into his job with Boeing, Michael was looking forward to retiring to spend more time with Becky and their five children. Both sets of parents were husbands, wives, fathers, and mothers by the time Sally and Tom married. That wasn't the only big difference. By the time that Michael and Becky had married, their parents had long since become good friends. Michael and Becky had each visited their future in-laws' homes at least four times. The same was true for Bob and Gena, as they both went to the same high school in Tallahassee when they began dating. The Schmitters and the Ratcliffs, meanwhile, met for the first time the week prior to their children's wedding.

Generational Differences

Things have changed since 1960. In 1960, the average age of first marriages in the Western world was 22.8 for men and 20.3 for women. The divorce rate was substantially lower than the 50+ per cent rate of today.[1] And even when young adults were single, they usually lived at home for the brief period of time between school and marriage and as such they generally stayed tied in to a family and a community. Today, about 50 per cent of adults in America are single and a good 40 per cent of them live away from home (either never having married, or having already divorced). In 2003, the average age of first marriage was over 28 for men and over 26 for women in America, Canada, and Japan. Add a year each for England, France, and two years for Germany, and Italy.[2] In short, young adults today marry later in life, and with less success.

Why is this the case? Some point to educational and technological trends. More people than ever are going to college (53 per cent increase since 1970).[2] Others argue that the collapse of the youth labor market is making it more difficult for people to gain a measure of financial independence. Still others point to the increased mobility made possible by technology – think not

1. This statistic means that, yes, slightly more than one out of every two marriages ends in divorce. However, it does not follow that one of every two married persons will experience a divorce. Divorcees often experience more than one divorce. There is some evidence that second marriages fail more often than first marriages. (For example, see Joshua R. Goldstein, "The Leveling of Divorce in the United States" *Demography* 36 (1999): 409-414; or Andrew Cherlin, *Marriage, Divorce, Remarriage* (Cambridge, MA: Harvard University Press, 1992)

2. See cover story "Grow Up? Not So Fast", by Lev Grossman, *Time Magazine*, January 24, 2005, pp. 42–54.

just lower prices for airfares, but the Internet and cell-phones giving shape to the idea of a "global community". Because of this global community, youth can have exponentially more options in terms of school, work/study abroad programs, internship programs where students spend their summers employed in the area of their chosen field (be it business, engineering, or architecture), vocational institutions, and the like. But can these economic factors really account for the effects in their entirety? If we go a bit farther back, we find some trends set in motion even before the 1950s that shed light on today's situation.

At the turn of the nineteenth century, it was customary for romantic interactions to take place within the sphere of the family, with recreation occurring within the home or among close friends (e.g. church socials). A man would come over to a woman's house (usually by invitation from the woman's parents, either with or apart from his initiation), be greeted by a servant, and admitted into a parlor where the woman would be waiting. She would play the piano for him or they would converse under the watchful eyes of her parents. This was often referred to as the "calling" system: a gentleman was coming over to "call" upon a lady.[3]

3. Beth L. Bailey, *From Front Porch to Back Seat, Courtship in Twentieth-Century America*, The John Hopkins University Press, 1989.

Sometime around the 1920s, the process of expressing interest in the opposite sex shifted from the private to the public arena. A man would still arrive at a woman's house, but she would commonly be wearing a hat – symbolizing that she was prepared to go out, usually into the world of commercial entertainment. The man worked; she didn't. Therefore, he paid; she didn't. But this assumption of a financial burden for the man was also accompanied by a shift in power. Since the man was paying, he gradually began to assume the right to make the invitation. So power shifted from the woman's family to the man.

But the shift from the private (the homes of families) to the public arena (theaters, restaurants) was equally important. The interactions were now taking place increasingly away from loved ones (family, close friends) and out in the domain of strangers in the public sphere. This inherently promoted a shift in the focus of the activity from group socialization and interaction for the express purpose of finding a life partner, to individual (the single man and woman) participation in activities chiefly intended to provide amusement and diversion.[4] It is not that in the private sphere

4. I do believe the "private to public" shift described was at least correlative if not causative of the shift in focus from getting married to being amused. The former context promoted responsibility, the latter context had far greater tolerance for irresponsibility. Note the nuanced language. It is not as though the latter intrinsically excludes responsibility.

individual couples did not enjoy themselves in the company of the opposite sex, it is simply that enjoyment wasn't the primary goal. Likewise, marriages were still formed when couples interacted by going out on the town, marriage was just not the main thing people were after by and large. The question was shifting from, "Is he/she the sort of person that would make a good husband/wife?" to "Did you have a good time?" Sexual promiscuity outside of marriage was still frowned upon, but chiefly because the "strangers" among whom premarital activities were occurring had themselves been raised in a milieu that gave allegiance to a Judeo-Christian heritage regarding sexual mores (and birth control and abortion were as yet uncommon). Another generation would soon rise up that did not presuppose such sexual convictions, and had easy access to contraceptives, and then a massive tide would shift. In the USA, we called it the sexual revolution.

But let's step back and examine the shift. In the system of "calling", the possibility (and hope) of marriage set the tenor of all interactions and the involvement of established families gave structural clarity to all participating parties. However, in the first half of the twentieth century, another shift was taking place – namely, the formation of a youth culture, as an increasing number of teenagers were continuing their education rather than immediately following in Mom or Dad's footsteps at the age of 13–14. Many movies (the entertainment industry was burgeoning at this time, as well as the media in general) were geared toward youth, and thus symbols of youth were being defined. Youth were increasingly characterized as "adolescents", and social theorists referred to adolescence as a particularly awkward stage in life, filled with special challenges.[5] We were told not to expect maturity and responsibility from adolescents, but rather rebelliousness, an adventurous spirit, and sexual experimentation. The system of dating that the youth practiced was (unlike the system of "calling") less about marriage and more about having a good time and being rewarded socially for one's popularity.

These trends continued into the second half of the twentieth century. College education gradually became the norm, as the economy increasingly required highly specialized skills. Careers became driven more by individuals than by couples and families. One hundred years ago, children were

5. According to a recent cover story in *Time Magazine*, the word "teenager" first appeared in print with a 1941 article in the periodical *Popular Science Monthly*. (See "Being 13", by Nancy Gibbs, *Time Magazine*, Time-Warner, August 8, 2005, pp. 40-44.)

literally (that is, economically) an asset to a family: they could contribute significant manual labor to a family's business, and care for their parents when they became elderly. Today, as a technology driven economy has emerged, children and even spouses can be a drag on the system. How so? If a married couple has children, one of them will likely need to greatly diminish their earning potential in order to care for the child. If they both keep working, then the day-care program costs money. If a man wants to have a career in London, but his wife is more drawn to opportunities in Scotland, at least one of them will have to make a sacrifice to not optimally pursue their economic usefulness. The present economy seems to value contributors as *individuals* rather than as married couples or families. This isn't to say that businesses are inherently trying to break families apart. It is simply that pure economics would dictate each individual working where their potential for output (i.e. economic benefit to society) is optimized. This may sound absurd, as few people are aware or intentional about this. Nevertheless, the trend of "commuter marriages" is on the rise.[6] The effect can be observed more subtly if one surveys 18–20 year-olds for what is the most pressing question that they face in

6. *Wandering Toward the Altar* by Ken Myers, Mars Hill Audio series.

the next five years. Their answer will very likely have to do with career considerations, like the need to select a major and obtain good grades, or longings for adventure such as travel and the like. Almost no student, male or female, would say that the most important decision that lay before them in the immediate future was the identification of a life partner and the consummation of such a relationship.[7]

Yet another trend that is contributing to the rise in the marriage age can be called *delayed adolescence*. The concept of a stage of adolescence for teenagers was developed in the early to mid 1900s; today we're seeing adolescence increasingly prolonged into the mid to late twenties or beyond.[8] The definition of adolescence by secular psychologists as a period of unproductive angst, during which teenagers are expected to rebel against all authorities and seek thrills without significant restraint, turned into a financial boon for the entertainment industry. If being young means having fun, and having fun means seeing movies or playing video games, or otherwise avoiding adult responsibilities, then it is in the interest of the entertainment industry

7. Kass and Kass, Chapter 1.

8. Sometimes this is now referred to as the "singles" culture. Again, the assumption is gradually accepted that such a young adult phase of irresponsibility is normal. Never mind that fact that this demographic statistically did not exist prior to 1950.

to push the boundaries at both ends. In other words, if 12–13-year-olds can be encouraged to start acting like "adolescents" even in their pre-teen years, so much the better. And from the perspective of the commercial entertainment industry, if 20-year-olds can be absolved of the need to become adults, then so be it. Today, it is not uncommon to see even 11-year-old girls trying to look like twentysomething Britney Spears or other pop stars. And on the other end, one can also find 30-year-olds riding skateboards while going to play video games.

Now add to this the fact that in the post-WWII era, discretionary income has grown. The "Greatest Generation[9]"(the term used by Tom Brokaw for the fifty million Americans born before 1945) raised their children with more affluence than they themselves experienced in their upbringing. And why not, wasn't that part of the American dream – to see one's children better off than you were at their age? So their children, marrying later, have doubly more discretionary income: not just what their parents provided for them, but what they themselves produce because they opt not to spend by delaying marriage and children. So luxury vacations, sports cars, movies, and entertainment are industries doing remarkably well today – and not

9. Tom Brokaw, *The Greatest Generation*, Random House, copyright 1998.

just because of retiring baby boomers. Their parents were very thrifty with their money following the Great Depression. They currently hold nearly two-thirds of all the nation's financial assets and will leave an estimated $38 trillion to their children. This will make the roughly eighty million Americans born between 1977 and 1997 the wealthiest generation in the history of the USA.[10]

As these culture shifts with regard to marriage and career have been occurring, the birth rate has not surprisingly been decreasing to historic lows. In the US, as of 2003, the number of births among women of ages 15–44 has declined by almost 50 per cent since 1960 to 66.9 births per year per 1,000 women. In Italy, the birth rate as of April 2004 is 1.23 per woman. Figures for France (1.26) and Germany (1.3) are likewise lower than the 2.1 needed to sustain the population. Spain has the lowest figure (1.07). A rising number of immigrants is currently filling the gap in these European countries. Government authorities have been admitting that these numbers are a cause for concern. In Italy, for example, Rocco Falivena, the mayor of Laviano, has offered 1000 euros to women who have a second child.[11]

10. Mark Driscoll, *Radical Reformission*, p. 194, Zondervan, copyright 2004.
11. Precise values depend on the source. This information is generally available on the Internet. Useful data can be found at www.infoplease.com/ipa/A0004395; www.globalagendamagazine.com/2004/adairturner.asp

The delay of marriage and the declining birth rate suggest that singles today in the Western world think of marriage in a fundamentally different way than their parents did. Historically, marriage has been an assumed necessity. For one, having children was how one's family name was perpetuated (which was seen as an honor). Secondly, the investment of one's energies, time, and income into children was considered a worthy pursuit. Thirdly, many family businesses depended on children. And fourthly, there was no government assistance for the health care and other economic needs of the elderly. When you got sick and old, it was your children who took care of you.

So how do singles envision marriage today? Often, primarily as an institution to bring about emotional fulfillment. This is why so many couples cohabit rather than (or before) marrying. That way, they can have the emotional fulfillment without all the paperwork (not to mention the hassle if things don't work out). This is also why our public discussion on same-sex marriage has become so politically viable (with Canada and some European countries adopting same-sex marriage laws). Take away the procreative aspect of marriage, and one man with one woman is no longer necessary. Why not two men? Or two women? Or even three women? The desire for emotional fulfillment often points inward – the longing to enhance *my* life. The desire for a fruitful union inherently points outward – the longing to give of myself to create and nurture life, in both my spouse and our children, and to (in a sense) pay back the gift of life by propagating the human race.

Aside from the issue of how singles view marriage and child-rearing, one thing that both Christian and non-Christian social thinkers agree upon is this: no other generation in Western culture has had so little structural framework of behavioral expectations in the process of premarital romantic interaction. Put it this way: if a man came to call upon a woman in 1880, everyone (the woman, the man, her family, his family, her friends, his friends) knew what that meant. Within the activity of the call, certain behavior was accepted, and other forms of behavior were socially forbidden. Now fast-forward sixty-five years to 1945. A man calls a woman and asks her if she'd like to attend the school dance with him. Again, this would have clear social expectations. Certain behavior would be appropriate for her, and also for him. And the same would be true if the woman called the man in 1945. Her behavior would have a particular connotation (rebellion) precisely because she would be acting contrary to cultural expectations.

But fast-forward seventy more years to 2005. Can you say, today, what it means if a middle-class 15-year-old girl picks up the phone and calls an older boy? Or how about if a 35-year-old woman offers a man her business card at a social gathering? To press the point even further, if you knew that two people slept together last week, would you be able to deduce how they define their relationship? The answer in each case is you would not, automatically, be able to assign meaning to these acts, for the individuals are acting outside any clearly defined structural framework. Hence, they must themselves assign meaning to these acts. In the words of Beth Bailey from whom these illustrations were taken, "The uncertainties are staggering, complicated enough for those who observe, possibly debilitating for those who participate."[12]

Go Back to the Good Old Days?

Many would see the above trends as vindicating their innate sense that the state of affairs in the world is inherently getting worse over time. "Bring back the good old days", they'd say, and everything would be just fine. "If only we could just keep all the singles living with their parents until they married." "If only we could just keep

12. Beth L. Bailey, *From Front Porch to Back Seat, Courtship in Twentieth-Century America*, John Hopkins University Press, 1989.

women from entering the workplace." "If only we just got rid of church youth groups." And so numerous conservative Christian countercultures have arisen seeking to take us back in time to "the good old days".

But here the Word of God would tell us: "Say not, 'Why were the former days better than these?' For it is not from wisdom that you ask this" (Eccles. 7:10). And again: "What has been is what will be, and what has been done is what will be done, and there is nothing new under the sun" (Eccles. 1:9). Man has been sinful since the dawn of time. Neither the automobile, the cellphone, nor the Internet, are inherently evil or good. Because of human depravity, they are often used as occasions of sin. And because of common grace, they are often used for much good. And a wise Christian will learn how to use them for much good as part of the dominion mandate given to man at creation (Gen. 1:28).

A nostalgic, "Why can't we have the good old days back again?" is unwarranted and misplaced. The factors that contributed to these cultural shifts described above are legion – and not all of them were expressly sinful. For example, the increasing need for education in the marketplace resulted in unmarried men and women spending more time together. It could not be avoided. As a people, we have developed technologically and economically in a manner that forbids our society to return. What we must do is seek to glean timeless, biblical principles and apply these even as the culture continues to change. We need to approach our culture as missionaries approach the cultures to which they are called and apply the gospel to our particular situation. This requires rigorous study of both the gospel and the culture, and it is indeed more difficult, because culture is changing faster than it has at many times in the past.

Thus, the challenge is to recognize that the issues Christian young people are facing in the area of singleness and sexuality are enormously difficult, but that efforts to bring back the golden years will often fall short of addressing the heart issues. In Chapter 2 we will be attempting to distinguish between biblical principles and methods that are negotiable and culturally dependent. We'll explore the difference between legalism and lawlessness in the area of dating and courtship. Chapters 3 and 4 will discuss the cultivation of biblical manhood and womanhood. We'll also talk about the equally important concept of learning to recognize and cultivate mature, robust, biblical manhood or womanhood in the opposite sex. Chapters 5 and 6 will conclude the book by discussing the practical matters associated with the choosing of a member of the opposite sex with whom to develop a relationship, as well as the premarital relationship process itself.

So getting back to Sally and Tom. Have they sinned because Tom didn't meet Sally by "calling" on her? That is, by visiting her in the parlor in her parents' home and interacting only within group settings? Are they locked into a second-rate marriage because they came from different hometowns and have large, disparate groups of friends? I hope you'll stay with us, because this book will address these sorts of questions. We'll see that the making of a strong marriage is indeed helped by a strong community, and that God's provision of community often can come in a variety of ways for those who value the body of Christ and take appropriate initiative. God's people need not be debilitated by the increase of choices (not least of all in the area of choosing a life partner) and mobility afforded by modern society.

It is my hope and prayer that for all those who have not yet experienced "the event" that Tom and Sally have, this book will be both helpful and encouraging. And for those already married that it will assist you in raising young men and women to have a high view of masculinity, femininity, and marriage. May our God be glorified as we seek to understand His Word in this area, so that we can make a generational impact for His kingdom. Soli deo Gloria.

Discussion Questions:

1. How have your dating experiences or expectations differed from what your parents experienced?

2. What changes over the past thirty years or so in how people date or court do you think have been positive? Or negative?

3. Does the concept of "delayed adolescence" ring true in your experience? What are some examples in your life, or that you have seen in others?

4. Were any of the statistics or history shared in the chapter surprising?

5. What does marriage mean for you? When you think of it, is marriage about emotional fulfillment? An option for financial security? A means to have sexual relations? An opportunity to raise children? Others?

6. What "uncertainties" about dating and male/female interactions have you felt or observed? What are some examples you have encountered?

2
The Normality of Marriage?

Introduction

In Chapter 1 we saw the differences between Tom and Sally's generation, and that of their parents, and I gave a bit of the history of how we got to where we are now. We attributed careerism, delayed adolescence (in some cases promoted by the commercial entertainment industry), and the rising youth culture to the apparent resistance to marriage and family evidenced today.

Now we will look at eight descriptions of how many of today's singles approach their singleness. Since all singles, like all married folk, are sinners, no one lives out singleness perfectly (except Christ), and many of these points will describe errors. And as we have discussed, our culture is presenting us with some particularly challenging circumstances. Even though none of these approaches might describe you perfectly or completely, prayerfully read this with a heart to discern what approach(es) might characterize you.

1. Are you approaching singleness too individualistically?

Do you find that you largely pursue romantic interests outside of a church or other structured community? Or is your community made up solely of peers, who are afraid or reluctant to ask hard questions of accountability? Are many of your romantic interactions without any clear cultural expectations either for the gender roles or for the process of romance?

2. Do you feel that you are entitled to happiness?

Many singles today have a stronger sense of this entitlement than those of prior generations did. This approach can lead to two conflicting approaches to singleness: given the influence of mainstream media, and especially the high divorce rate, you may be more likely to associate marriage with misery and strife. So you steer clear of it, avoiding it indefinitely. On the other hand, you may strongly desire marriage, yet reject every close relationship with potential, because you have a sense that the other person doesn't quite meet all your needs, the relationship doesn't feel "just right", or you have unrealistic standards that the other person cannot meet.

3. Are you passive in your pursuit of a marriage partner?

This tendency can result from both the first two points. This is particularly the case for men, but is increasingly observed in women as well. Whereas prior generations anticipated making sacrifices to achieve the personal fulfillment of marriage and family, many of you may experience relational commitment in a more reactionary manner. It is something that happens to you, perhaps surprisingly, and then you must adjust. This is often accompanied by an inability to "pull the trigger" and settle on a lifemate because a subjective set of feelings is lacking, you don't think you're old enough, or haven't had enough fun to settle down yet.

4. Are you afraid to lose the security of singleness?

This may surprise you, but I am especially referring to women who strongly desire to get married, who may have been single for a long time, or who may have been deeply wounded in a past relationship. The longer we are single, the more settled we become. We know how to live single, and the thought of embarking on an intimate, committed relationship can really rock the boat, even if it is one of our deepest desires. Are you (even if unintentionally) sabotaging potential romances in order to hold on to the life you know?

5. Do you not feel ready yet for marriage?

This is a highly appropriate attitude if you are 15. But perhaps you are 35 and pursuing your second graduate degree. We'll talk further in this chapter about the wisdom of considering marriage and family to be a key ingredient of adulthood. While it is becoming more normal to delay marriage until the education, career, travel plans, and retirement portfolio are all tied up in a neat little bow, delays of this type can be related more to immaturity and laziness than wise foresight. And if you are waiting to become the perfect spouse or become perfectly holy before you marry, it is best to drop that ambition. With this goal, you would never get married. And even if you were successful in your endeavors, you would certainly never find a perfect spouse for your perfect self!

6. Are you failing to pursue marriage in the right ways?

You may be ready for marriage, eager to get married, even heavily involved in a church singles' group and wondering where ARE all the eligible bachelors and bachelorettes? But there may be several ways in which you are jeopardizing yourself. Are you at a weaker church where there are few godly singles of the caliber you'd like to marry? Are you so involved in teaching 1st grade Sunday school that you are missing opportunities to interact with other adults? Are you looking for Christian singles in all the wrong places (like bars)? Are you spending 10–12 hours a day at work, plus putting in extra time on the weekends? Or have you racked up burdensome financial debt, which now greatly curbs your freedom (Prov. 22:7), or leaves you tied to Mom and Dad? Perhaps you believe that finding a spouse, unlike finding a job or obtaining groceries to fill your fridge, depends entirely on God and you have no role at all: "I shouldn't do anything because God will bring a spouse to me." If you are dating weaker or non-Christians just for companionship "in the meantime", you're also making yourself unavailable for marriage.

7. **Do you focus too much on finding someone rather than becoming someone?**
It's easy to spend all your energy worrying about what you want in a spouse or if you'll ever find one. In Chapters 3 and 4 we'll explore at length a topic that may be of much greater importance to you... what kind of person (and possibly spouse) God is calling you to become.

8. **Are you gifted with celibacy?**
Do you feel called by God to live celibately for your entire life? Are you content, and don't struggle much (or at all) with the desire for sex? You are blessed, and rare. This book will not have much that is directly relevant for you, but I pray that you will find help in the book as you counsel and encourage those in your life who are eager to marry (or are sinfully avoiding marriage).

Regardless of our inclinations on the subject of singleness and marriage, we may be tempted to go back to the structured processes and cultural expectations of past generations, but we must resist. Such sentiments are often, to borrow from another, a masked appeal for reactionary conservatism combined with intellectual laziness.[1] We do need to rid ourselves of much of what is wrong in our approach to marriage, but a focus on external methods (like mandating that a young man ask a woman's biological father for permission to pursue her) or circumstances (requiring that all women live with their parents until marriage) is ultimately not helpful. It can lead to judging others on the basis of man-made rules that go beyond the Bible's teaching. Others may become inclined to inaccurately associate their adherence to such rules as a sign of spirituality. Lastly, a misplaced focus on externals might hide rebellion only until the young people leave home.

Christians will always struggle to know where to draw the line between biblical principles and optional (cultural or situational) methods. In a society with almost no agreed-upon framework for premarital relationships, the temptation to force-fit a simple one-size-fits-all structure is present now more than ever. Likewise, there are also those who are content to swim along with the culture and trust that all will work out in the

1 D.A. Carson, *Becoming Conversant with the Emerging Church*, Zondervan, 2005.

end. Thoughtful Christians should seek to avoid either extreme.

Youthful tendencies need to be focused in a purposeful direction. Let's think about this in terms of age, gender, and life station. Not everything that makes sense for a 25-year-old will make sense for a 15-year-old. Likewise, not all actions and responsibilities that apply to a man will make sense for a woman, since a man has a unique responsibility to initiate. We'll return to this theme later.

One trend we need to deal with is that youth seem to be maturing faster, but with a concept of adulthood that includes recreation and fun, but not responsibility. While it is true that the on-set of puberty is occurring at a lower age today than in previous generations, what I'm referring to has manifestations beyond the transition to physical adulthood. I am talking about the fact that 12–13-year-olds find it "cool" to listen to the music of older teenagers, to hang out with older crowds, to drink and do drugs, or to spend the money and have the sort of freedoms that older teens enjoy. In a culture that values attractiveness, even prepubescent girls want to wear just the right bikini at the beach, particularly if they've noticed that older girls (if not boys) pay attention to such things.

And so there is also a race to enter the world of dating. You've probably seen this (or experienced it) – two 14-year-olds walking down the street hand-in-hand. What's wrong, you may say? Mere puppy love, is it not? The difficulty is that if you are already stoking the flames of hormonal passions at the age of 14, it is going to be very difficult to remain self-controlled until an age when marriage is possible. Further, physical intimacy clouds judgment, causing an intense emotional bond before two people really know each other. Then there is heartache at the breakup that could have been avoided.

Christian maturity recognizes that strong sexual passion leads inevitably either to marriage or to sin. So the possibility (and even probability) of marriage must be the backdrop that hangs over any romantic interaction. As Christians, we must be the people who unambiguously declare that marriage is the context for all sexual expression, the only possible condition for its fulfillment. This means that there needs to be the cultivation of, and respect for, mature expressions of masculinity and femininity that are in and of themselves winsome before God, and in marriage, valuable for companionship, mutual enjoyment, and working together as fellow heirs of the grace of life.

Since marriages are often occurring later in life today, and children are growing up faster, the time during which young people have active sex hormones and no biblically sanctioned outlet has been significantly extended. Add to this the fact that the habits of young people are often no different than those of the world (attending pubs and nightclubs, etc.), and so it's not surprising that the frequency of fornication is often no different among Christian young people than it is of non-Christian youth.[2] Where there is not fornication there is often intense sexual frustration (including struggles with pornography) that could be readily avoided by marriage.[3]

There need not be this extended period of time where youth must live as single, biological adults. People often protest, "Yes, but if they got married sooner, such marriages would more likely lead to divorce." It may be true that, today, those who marry when they are quite young (19–22) are more likely to divorce.[4] However, the fact that *immature* youth choose to marry early, and are

2. See, for example, the studies cited by Lauren Winner in "3 Fibs and a Truth about Sex", *Christianity Today*, Leadership Journal, Spring 2005, available at: http://www.christianitytoday.com/le/2005/002/15.50.html.

3. This is not to say that marriage intrinsically solves all problems stemming from a lack of sexual self-control. It is to say that, biblically, God anticipated such problems and created a safe environment for healthy sexual expression. To not accept marriage can thus be a failure to receive one of God's good gifts provided for your sanctification and protection.

4. Albert Y. Hsu, *Singles at the Crossroads*, InterVarsity Press, 1997, p. 19.

unsuccessful, does not prove that all who marry at a young age must experience the same fate. The problem is immaturity, not "early" marriages. Rather, if maturity is formed in youth during the teen years, marriages for young adults (when people begin to live apart from parents and assume financial responsibility for their own life) can be readily sustained.[5] And an important part of forming this sort of maturity in youth is the teaching of the normalcy of marriage for adults. Since it is so crucial that Christians conduct their romantic activities in the light of a potential marriage, we'll devote the rest of Chapter 2 to defending the normalcy of marriage for the adult. Later in this book we'll return to the theme of how young people can direct their passions toward marriage in a God-honoring fashion.

The Normality of Marriage

Lev Grossman noted that thirty years ago the category "single adult" was almost unnecessary.[6] Twenty and thirtysomethings, living on their own, hopping to different jobs and moving from town to town, were a nonexistent category, statistically

5. Such couples upon marriage do not need to unlearn habits that are developed in the single years during which their responsibilities towards their roommates or friends were not nearly on par with their new responsibilities to their spouse.

6. Lev Grossman, "Grow Up? Not So Fast", *Time*, January 24, 2005, 42–54. This very helpful study shows the statistics for the average age of first marriage for men and women in numerous Western countries.

speaking. Singles now constitute roughly 50 per cent of Western nations. It is likely that within a generation most people will spend the majority of their earthly life as singles (including divorces and the death of a spouse). Consequently, our youth are growing up in a milieu that suggests marriage is at best just one option among many for emotional fulfillment. That is why I feel it is appropriate to spend some time discussing the normality of marriage.

In Genesis 2:18, God has created man and now He famously declares, "It is not good that the man should be alone." Though this statement has implications beyond marriage, it seems to at least include marriage. Immediately after God declares that it is not good for man to be alone we're told, somewhat oddly, "So out of the ground the Lord God formed every beast of the field and every bird of the heavens and brought them to the man to see what he would call them. And whatever the man called every living creature, that was its name." The man then proceeds to name the animals. Why do we have this discussion occurring immediately after God's acknowledgment that the man should not be alone? It seems, at least on the surface, to be out of place. Others have argued, and I think persuasively, that at least part of God's intention was to reveal to Adam that which is noted in verse 20: "But for Adam there was not found a helper fit for him."[7] So Adam was made to recognize the truth that God had previously declared – he needs a helper, and has not found one yet. Then God creates Eve and Adam recognizes that this need is now met.

Throughout history, except in times of war or natural disaster, marriage has been the typical lot of an adult, regardless of race, culture, or religion.[8] In this sense, we can safely say that marriage (rather than singleness) was the norm. To balance this, however, we need to deal fairly with 1 Corinthians 7, where the Apostle Paul seems to prefer singleness. It should be noted that Paul's statement in verse 1 is probably a quote that the Corinthians made in a letter to him. Namely, "It is good for a man not to touch a woman." Paul affirms this, but qualifies it with verse 2: because of the (assumedly widespread) temptation to sexual immorality, each man should have his own wife and each woman her own husband. This qualification sounds like the one Jesus made in response to His disciples' statement that it was better not to marry. Not dismissing their remark, Jesus replied, "Not everyone can receive this saying, but only those

7. See Douglas Wilson, for example, *Reforming Marriage*, Canon Press, 1995.
8. See also, for example, the chapter by Albert Mohler in *Sex and the Supremacy of Christ*, edited by John Piper and Justin Taylor, Crossway, 2005.

to whom it is given" (Matt. 19:10-11). Certainly, later in 1 Corinthians 7 Paul does reveal his own preference that singles remain single, because it offers peculiar opportunities for kingdom ministry. Yet the implication of the passage as a whole suggests that such individuals possess, to quote Calvin, "a gift by a *special* grace of God" (Calvin's Geneva study Bible, emphasis mine).

The upshot of this is that if you are single, you should be giving yourself with particular earnestness to ministry that extends the kingdom of God. You have the freedom to go and come as you please, but you should use it not for yourself, but for others to the glory of God. You are a gift to God's church. Use it well, as one who will have to give an account. Pastors and church leaders, likewise, should receive such Christians with open arms as gifts to the church.

That said, if you are an adult single, do consider if you may be uniquely gifted for singleness. If you are, it will be evidenced in part by a lack of desire for sexual companionship, which would allow you, without undue discomfort, to forgo marital bliss for a lifetime. And my guess is that if you're in that group, you are probably not reading this book (at least for yourself)! But for most, you probably find sexual purity to be significantly challenging and either an occasion for sinfulness or frustration. And for you, marriage should be the focus of your premarital romantic activity. In fact, to a large degree, marriage will mark your transition to adulthood in the fullest sense – because it is in the joys and sufferings of marriage that God will sanctify you into the person you could not possibly become apart from marriage. This book is primarily written for you, your pastors, and your parents.

I know there are numerous objections to what I have said, so I want to deal with them one by one to make sure I am not misunderstood.

Objection #1: *If what you are saying is true, how would I know if I possess this "gift by a special grace of God" or if in fact I should seek marriage?* From Scripture, the primary indicator would be a level of contentment with celibacy. If instead there is an urgent longing for sexual satisfaction or emotional intimacy, marriage should be considered. You may legitimately wait until an educational or vocational program is completed so that you can be financially independent from your parents, or you may delay marriage to become better acquainted with the sort of person you should marry. These good considerations notwithstanding, unless you are gifted with celibacy you should prepare for the future with marriage in mind.

Objection #2: What if I am the sort of person described above who should plan for marriage, but God just hasn't brought that special person into my life?

This objection can seem remarkably legitimate, but it's wise to do some soul searching first before settling for this explanation.

The first response I'd make is: What are you doing to become the sort of person who would be winsome and attractive to the kind of person you want to marry? In other words, say you want to marry someone godly, charming, outgoing, and others-oriented. Well, are you developing godliness, charisma, and a servant's heart? If not, don't be surprised if godly members of the opposite sex are not showing interest in you.

Next, what type of standards do you have for someone of the opposite sex? One common experience of older singles is that as each successive year of singleness accrues, the standards of a "suitable mate" actually increase. This may seem counterintuitive; and some singles may claim otherwise. "I'll take anyone at this point", they may say. However, the more people they date, or see, or know, the more they can compare a particular person to someone "out there" who they think is better. For example, Joe has dated five girls and each was missing something in particular. He starts dating a sixth girl, who seems great, but now she's missing that wonderfully salient quality that girl #2 had (who had been rejected because she lacked the good looks of girl #1). So he tells himself, "Girl number seven will be perfect!" And he continues on his search. Given the mobility of modern life, who knows? In a few months, he might find someone in another town and she might be "the one". The reality is, however, that the number of single Christian women he's meeting is bound to decrease every year if for no other reason than that they are marrying off and that it becomes more impractical (and therefore unlikely) to meet many of them in one place, such as college ministry or some other shared experience.

It is noteworthy that women more frequently make this objection – that the right man has not yet pursued them. Women do have a unique responsibility to respond to, nurture, and affirm male initiation in this area, and the last thing I'd want to do is make a woman feel guilty for being committed to doing so. That said, women can also (perhaps unwittingly) make the mistake of setting unrealistic expectations. Many women, for example, believe that there must be one "perfect match" for them out there, and it's their job to wait for him. This may seem romantic, but it is horribly debilitating. As soon as she's lost that first rush of emotion and is getting to know him as a flawed human (and not the paragon of perfection her ignorance initially allowed him to be) she feels obligated to end the relationship. This happens with some frequency where women have been duped by the media into thinking that marriage must be a state of perpetual bliss and that, if it is not, something must be wrong with their partner. Such a mentality, if learned during the single years, can be devastating in marriage. Such discontent singles make discontent husbands and wives. A theological sidebar: though God does providentially orchestrate our lives, a mystical theology that suggests we can discover God's secret will is bound to frustrate. Who we marry falls into the realm of God's secret (unrevealed) will (Deut. 29:29). There is a "specific person" out there, but we only find out who it is by obeying the principles God has revealed in His Word, making our vows, and walking down the aisle.[9]

Lastly, some folk who make this objection (men and women) are doing very little to put themselves in the path of godly members of the opposite sex who are probably marriage-minded and could make a suitable match. They may work too many hours or spend unreasonable amounts of

9. See Friesen, *Decision Making and the Will of God.*

time on hobbies that don't promote fellowship. If you are giving all your energy and time to worldly activities, worldly people are whom you are likely to attract. Single Christians who are taking advantage of their season in life for undistracted devotion to the Lord (as Paul urges them to) will be giving their time and energy to ministries that bless others, and the sort of man or woman they hope to marry will be doing the same. If you are running hard after God, He may open your eyes to the worthiness of someone running right alongside you.

But you say, "I've carefully considered all you say, and I am not falling into any of these errors, and I'm still single. Why?" The balance is that God does not promise us we will be married, and we are called to be content in whatever circumstances we are in (Phil. 4:11). I pray that you will be engaged in service to your local church, using your singleness for His glory, and continuing to grow and develop the personality, godliness, and skills that will make you an excellent spouse, and that He will give you deep and abiding contentment in this season which may last a few months or a lifetime. God may have a plan for glorifying Himself through your singleness that goes far beyond anything you can imagine. Trust Him to work out all things for your good and His glory in the end.

Objection #3: *Doesn't this way of thinking cause me to look down on my single friends, particularly the older ones?*

Since we're not God, we cannot know all the reasons for their singleness. Hence, as we interact with them, we may discover areas of their life that we may challenge (these sorts of conversations should be going on all the time in healthy churches), we may come alongside them and comfort them as they rely on God for contentment, or (alternatively) we may be in a position to encourage them to consider whether singleness may in fact be God's special gifting for them.

Objection #4: *Does this mean that if I'm still single, I am less than who God is calling me to be and I cannot be sanctified?*

Absolutely not; Christ was not less than perfect, and the great apostle, Paul, was most likely single. Cherish the season God has you in and trust that He will use you and perfect you (Rom. 8:28) regardless of your marital status. But be diligent in discerning if you do have any areas of growth or error that might be keeping you unnecessarily from marriage.

Objection #5: _What steps can a single woman take to find a husband, if she's convinced from the Bible and her conscience that it's a man's responsibility to take initiative?_

This is an excellent question, and probably one that many of you were thinking about. To a large extent, the prolonged single years of women are the result of the sins of passive men. Namely, men who won't grow up, take initiative and responsibility, find the woman God would have them marry, and raise children to the glory of God. That is why most of my exhortation has been to the men.

Women, nevertheless, need to continue to cultivate contentment in their single years. They can pray. They can continue developing their femininity in whatever providences they experience as single women (work, hobbies, church activities, etc.). Such femininity will be attractive to a masculine, godly man. They can develop a nurturing disposition through volunteer baby-sitting (for example) and other involvements with younger women or children. They can learn to be content with their wages and resist the lure of the corporate ladder.

Secondly, it is possible to look for a husband without hunting for one. For example, it may be wise for a woman to move to a place where there is a strong, larger church with elders who can know her and care for her, and where she may meet more available Christian, godly men. At this point, I should also note that it is possible for a woman to have an inordinate desire to marry at a young age to escape the responsibilities of life or to perhaps become free from parents with whom she may be quarreling. This sometimes happens in the case of a young woman from a troubled home. However, to the contrary, her problems will not be alleviated with marriage. Such a woman probably has trouble with authority in her life, and will likely bring her husband much grief.

This principle can be generalized to more than just young women from troubled homes. For both men and women, an inordinate desire for marriage may be indicative of general discontentment. *We need to be able to distinguish between a healthy and an unhealthy discontentment*. Since God intends that most singles marry, some degree of discontentment with the state of singleness is inevitable for these (most) singles. It is what propels them to marry. However, where there is unhealthy discontentment, people are making an idol out of marriage. As we noted earlier, some think of marriage as an institution of perpetual bliss. Conversely, a healthy discontentment with singleness maintains a biblical, realistic view of marriage. Such a man or woman wishes to embrace the challenges of marriage for the glory of God and for their sanctification. Indeed, they ought to look to marriage as an opportunity to have God reveal to them degrees of their own selfishness and pride that were otherwise unknown. Marriage becomes the necessary crucible for sanctification for these people. I said to my wife on my wedding day, "I cannot become the man God means for me to become apart from you." I still believe that was a true statement.

OK, shifting gears a bit, what should our response be, if we've accepted the idea that marriage is the norm for Christian adults? Well, naturally, we will want to find someone we want to marry, and this gives purpose and direction to our romantic interests. However, as I alluded to earlier in response to objection #2, we must focus on the one person for whom God will hold us responsible: **ourselves**. The scriptural emphasis is on working out **our** salvation with fear and trembling (by God's grace!), becoming the sort of person God intends for us to become. Consequently, to emphasize how to find someone would be putting the cart before the horse. In one sense, we continue to "become" even after we've "found", so I'm not suggesting one has to wait until he is "perfectly mature as a single" in order to get married. (This would discourage all of us, and we'd never marry!) Rather, as we give emphasis to growing in the grace of God (becoming), we trust God for our active finding of a spouse in His timing. And this "trust" will look different in a man than in a woman. We'll look at that in a later chapter.

Discussion questions:

1. Did any of the eight struggles of singleness resonate with you? Which do you see in your life?

2. What do you think about the "gift of celibacy"? Do you have it? Can you think of anyone you know who does? Do you agree with how the chapter defines it? Go to 1 Corinthians 7 to investigate further.

3. Were you surprised to learn that the frequency of fornication is just as high among Christian youth? What are some reasons for this? How can you combat this in your life, and in the lives of other Christians?

4. Discuss the "normality of marriage", given the fact that neither Jesus nor Paul was married. What implications does this have for those who are young and eager to marry? Those who prefer not to marry? Those who have longed to marry and now are in their forties or fifties?

5. What role do you think a woman can/should play in pursuing marriage? Has this chapter challenged or supported your thinking? What are some other ways a woman can make herself available to godly men without hunting them?

6. How can you both trust God for a spouse, and be looking for one at the same time? Are these mutually exclusive?

degree, or the landing of a stable job. This mind-set is the outworking of a cultural worldview that places too much emphasis on individualism and career. Rather, a man should conceive of his adulthood not just in relation to his work, but also in relation to maturity in his spiritual life. The latter is accurately measured (among other criteria) by whether there is sufficient maturity to lead a wife and children, to be a responsible husband and father, and to work hard not just for himself but also for the good of others. In many ways, marriage and fatherhood place unique stresses on a man and so become a crucible for his sanctification. That said, there is a certain amount of foundational maturity that a man (and a woman) ought to bring into marriage, and this foundational maturity flows primarily from an understanding and demonstration of biblical masculinity and femininity. Manhood is where boyhood should be aimed and womanhood is where girlhood should be aimed.

Defining Biblical Masculinity

Douglas Wilson helpfully sets forth concepts of masculinity in his book *Future Men*.[1] Wilson quotes Douglas Jones' definition of masculinity: "the collection of all those characteristics which

1. Douglas Wilson, *Future Men*, Canon Press (2001).

flow from delighting in and sacrificing bodily strength for goodness". This conjures images of soldiers training to fight a noble battle. Wilson includes Bill Mouser's expansion upon this concept by pointing to five aspects of masculinity: (1)exercising of dominion over the earth, (2)exercising stewardship, making the world flourish, (3)becoming saviors, delivering others, (4)growing in wisdom, becoming sages, and (5)reflecting the image and glory of God. Mouser submits that these traits can be summarized in five words: *lord*, *husband*, *savior*, *sage*, and *glory-bearer*.

A *lord* exercises dominion. We saw in the Genesis account that God gave Adam dominion in the Garden of Eden. In our day, a man demonstrates lordship by diligently pursuing his areas of giftedness and interest, developing skills and a career – in law, medicine, business, engineering, astrophysics, journalism, auto maintenance, creative writing, music, art, etc. As he develops his gifts, he makes new contributions to a field and expands the capability of mankind. This is good and right; God made man to rule over the created order, to understand it, and thus gain mastery over it.

The derivation of the word *husband* comes from agriculture and refers to the cultivation of plants or animals. A husband is one who develops fruitfulness through careful stewardship. He is to do this in a home, with a wife, whose loveliness he cultivates by the way he treats her, and he is to do this with his possessions. A lord makes scientific discoveries, goes to the moon, or starts a new business; a husband settles down after these conquests, maintains them, and makes improvements. He may write scientific papers, hire accountants for his business, or learn to do auto repair work in a more efficient manner to optimize his profits. He may clean his garage and repair the broken dishwasher, or sand the deck so his kids don't get splinters. He will take his wife on dates to nurture their relationship. A husband takes care of things; he does not let them fall into disarray. He is active and intentional, and he assumes responsibility for what's under his stewardship.

In his duties as a husband a man takes care of what's his; in his office of *savior* he seeks to give of himself for others. Boys naturally gravitate to stories like David and Goliath in the Bible. They love stories of dragons slayed by brave and noble knights. From an early age, boys will play by wrestling, by pretend sword fighting, and with toy guns. Many parents fear such activities, but they really shouldn't. To be sure, a boy may on occasion exert his aggression without self-control, but such aggression must be channeled, not smothered. While a student, former US President Theodore Roosevelt taught Sunday school. A boy arrived with a black eye, admitting he had been in a fight. The boy explained that a bigger boy had been pinching his sister, so he fought him. The future President gave him a dollar for his bravery, but was promptly relieved from his duties by the church. No doubt there was probably some rashness in the boy for starting a fight so easily, but the instinct to save others from evil must be commended to prevent the boy from growing up with a stunted view of manhood. There are numerous recent best-selling books in America that have recovered this notion that men need something compelling to live and die for. The very fact that they sold well speaks to the widespread decline of masculinity in our culture and the unconscious, deep-seated need of men to connect with this aspect of how God made them. Boys must learn to be strong, sacrificial, courageous, and to give themselves for what is right, regardless of how difficult that path may be.

A boy is to grow into a *sage*. Discipline in studies does not come easily for boys or girls, but it can seem particularly difficult for boys. Boys need to be taught that it is masculine to do well in school. Such training will be essential for his roles as lord and husband. But by sage we refer to something more (not less) than excellence in the classroom. A boy should repeatedly read the book of Proverbs, and should seek for wisdom like silver (Prov. 2). He should regularly learn lessons from the sluggard(Prov. 10:26), from the one seduced by the adulteress(Prov. 7) and from the fool who speaks rashly like sword thrusts (Prov. 12:18). Last, but not least, the Proverbs will teach him to not waste all his time and money chasing girls,[2] but to recognize and pursue an excellent wife (Prov. 1).

The degree to which a man (or boy) exhibits mature, robust masculinity will depend first on his relationship with God. He is to understand that masculinity finds its perfect example in the Lord Jesus Christ, who grew in wisdom and stature while being obedient to His parents, who taught and trained His disciples faithfully, both in word and by example, and who cared for His mother even while giving His life for the salvation of the world. He is to step up to the challenge and risk of taking leadership, secure in his trust and reliance on both the person and the example of

2. I take that as the meaning of "Do not give your strength to women" (Prov. 31:3). The contrast, it seems, is with the fool, who is ensnared by the adulteress woman.

Christ. So mature masculinity is demonstrated by reflecting the glory (as a *glory-bearer*) of God through a faith that clings to Christ alone for salvation, that submits to the lordship of Christ in all areas of life, and that embraces Christ as the supreme treasure, of higher value than all the world (Matt. 13:41; Phil. 3:6-8).

Defining Biblical Femininity

It is unfortunate that too often in the church the *only* model for femininity articulated is that of the godly wife and mother. This could lead some to the false implication that marriage is necessary to experience full womanhood. Yet the traits described in the Proverbs 31 woman (who is a wife and mother) are, in context, the example of what a young man should look for in a potential wife, and so they can be developed and exhibited by single women as well (few women magically inherit all these characteristics as they walk down the aisle!). Let's consider a few of the traits of the Proverbs 31 woman: *hospitable, ingenious, hardworking, wise,* and *secure.*

The Proverbs 31 woman is *hospitable*; she enhances and beautifies the life of others. She gives comfort to the weary and the downtrodden. This is a woman whose orientation is directed outward, so that she is available to pour out her life for the good of those in her midst. Her schedule reflects the priority in her life of people – those in her church, non-Christians to whom she's ministering, the poor, her family. She's the sort that volunteers to play hostess at a larger get-together, so that the homeowners can more freely mingle with their guests or watch over their children. When she baby-sits, she is completely trustworthy. She is likely to take initiative with her friends by inviting others to group events, helping people feel included, and allowing others to borrow her possessions.

The Proverbs 31 woman is *ingenious*. Merriam-Webster defines ingenious as, "marked by originality, resourcefulness, and cleverness in conception or execution". Notice how this woman cultivates her property (the field she has bought), and works with her hands to take wool and flax and turn it into useful clothing. Women who are resourceful in one area soon learn how to be resourceful in many other areas. Such women can take negative situations and make something marvelous out of them. Rather than complaining and being anxious at their circumstances, Proverbs 31 women set to work at making things lovely (whether it be their home, an article of clothing, a meal, or a technical report) in a cheerful, warm manner.

The Proverbs 31 woman is *hardworking*. She is not someone who starts a large project, only to get distracted and decide it was not worthwhile. She is not the sort that only pursues rest and recreation – she does not want to lead a life of ease, away from the blessed duties of love to God and neighbor. She regularly asks herself, "How can I discipline my labors to do the most good in this world with the gifts, strengths, and passions God has given me?" Such a woman could not wallow long in loneliness over her singleness – she will be too busy doing good.

The Proverbs 31 woman is *wise*. "She opens her mouth with wisdom, and the teaching of kindness is on her tongue." She is not given to speaking rashly on the impulse of the moment. She considers her speech, and uses the power of her tongue to give a blessing. This will be exhibited both in diplomacy with acquaintances less socially adept, and in her ability to move conversations in directions that are uplifting and make others feel valued. Her wisdom is imparted to suffering or less mature Christian women, as well as non-Christian women with whom she builds long-term friendships with an eye toward winning their souls. Given the business savvy exhibited by the Proverbs 31 woman, I picture her wisdom as broad, encompassing interpersonal issues and business and life skills alike.

And finally the Proverbs 31 woman is *secure*. "[S]he laughs at the time to come." She is confidently delighting in God's provision for her needs as He deems best, knowing that God's purposes are far more limitless than she can imagine. As a single woman, this allows her to be content, trusting in God's wisdom. As a married woman, this allows her to lovingly affirm and support her husband's leadership and not be anxious regarding the future, her husband, or her children.

Femininity is also often described and demonstrated in relation to masculinity. Under such circumstances, if you define the moves of one dancer, you have defined the moves of the other. We live in a world that frequently tells us that any such discussion is "sexist", yet I would submit that the pattern of humble, servant, tender, strong, initiating male leadership and affirming, nurturing, joy-filled female responsiveness is not only the pattern of Scripture, but it is written on the heart of every human being on this globe. When women see the kind of masculinity I've described above, they generally will naturally respond to it with affirmation. What prevents mature masculinity and an affirming response is, in both cases, sinful human hearts.

John Piper and Wayne Grudem define femininity this way:

> At the heart of mature femininity is a freeing
> disposition to affirm, receive and nurture strength
> and leadership from worthy men in ways appropriate
> to woman's differing relationships.[3]

This definition speaks to a disposition. The disposition can be cultivated and even thrive *in the absence of a significant relationship with a man*. That said, let's unpack a few terms – *affirm*, *receive*, and *nurture*.

An *affirming* disposition is one that praises that which is praiseworthy in others. It validates worthiness and thus spurs others to behave in a worthy manner. It is amazing how much power a woman can exert over a man merely by affirming certain actions, words, and attitudes, and not others. A woman should take pains to develop an affirming disposition, rather than either frequently criticizing and complaining, or bragging and gloating to establish herself as the center of attention.

A *receiving* disposition is one that accepts the strength and leadership offered by worthy men. She is glad when he is not passive, and she does not want to reverse their roles. She feels enhanced, honored, and freed by his caring strength and

3. John Piper and Wayne Grudem, *Recovering Biblical Manhood and Womanhood: A Response to Evangelical Feminism*, Crossway, 1991, p. 46.

servant leadership. In practical matters, she feels honored by a man holding a door for her, or offering to walk her to her car late in the evening; she doesn't chafe at such treatment. The issue is not whether she is capable of doing a particular task (e.g. open a door) herself. She recognizes that it is appropriate that men show her honor, as a weaker vessel, because if they didn't, she'd be competing with men in everything, and, in God's wisdom, she was not made to do so. This is why, incidentally, some of the most "liberated" women (those with the least regard for the matters we've been discussing) are often among the most confused and insecure women. Conversely, women who know how to receive and nurture the strength of worthy men do not seek to be men themselves, and consequently have more joy, contentment, peace, and emotional security. The key to enjoying such peace is to trust God: that He is greater than any mistake a man can make in his leadership and that it is God's design that she affirm a man's leadership, even as it is expressed in imperfect or nascent form.

A *nurturing* disposition goes one step beyond *receiving*. Nurturing actually augments that which it receives – that is, it causes the strength and leadership received from worthy men to be enhanced. Again, this is a subtle way that women exert more power over men than they may recognize. In a mother, nurturing is what gives and sustains life, particularly to very young children. And nurturing is what shapes the life of young people in their early and late teen years, remarkably affecting the trajectory of their life into adulthood. This is the nature of the "suitable helper" described in Genesis 2:18, and of the life-giver the woman's body is uniquely fashioned to be.

The degree to which a woman (or girl) exhibits mature, robust femininity will depend first on her relationship with God. A woman who knows God at a deep level is most free to see that her personhood is made to complement that of men. She is free to be relationally oriented and does not find her worth in striving to approximate masculine behavior, attitudes, and life-disposition. She is glad to be a woman, and is secure in the way God made her and in the important role He gave her. She can receive honor from worthy men and can nurture and affirm noble, risk-taking, leadership from them. She feels special when treated that way and is unashamed to admit it. She can love others, including trustworthy (though fallible) men, and stand by her man in marriage.

Our culture has effeminized men, but equally dangerous has been the war against women.

Society despises truly feminine women. Women are told that their only worth will come from success in the marketplace, so that even though many prefer to be married with children, they are reluctant to admit it in academic and work environments. Consequently, there are far more women wanting to be treated like men than vice versa. So it is, at the core, womanhood itself that is disparaged. Women either feel stupid for wanting to be wives and mothers, or they pursue success in the same way as men and then wonder why they are unfulfilled. They increasingly cannot find a good man to marry because men are accustomed to treating them as "equals" (and enjoying the worldly fruits of a dual-income family) and so deny them the honor they are due, which would enhance their femininity and make them both happier and lovelier. Yet a strong, feminine woman will only give herself to a man who treats her with appropriate honor. Such a woman is therefore more secure and more fulfilled than "liberated" women.

A note of warning must be made at this point. The Bible does not teach that *all* women are to submit to *all* men. The Bible teaches that she is to submit only to her husband. So she is to marry a man who, by God's grace, is able to lead her. But she can still treat other men (before and after marriage) in a manner that encourages them in their God-given role of leadership. Her demeanor and attitude toward them, her demonstration of respect and affirmation, can go a long way toward building them up as masculine men. This doesn't mean she cannot give a contradictory opinion or exhibit a healthy degree of assertiveness in the workplace. It means that when she must do so, her attitude will nevertheless affirm his God-given penchant to demonstrate servant leadership.

An appreciation of the beauty of masculinity and femininity is at the heart of a vibrant society and church. Mature masculinity and femininity are foundational for single young men and women preparing themselves for marriage. Without this foundation, young men and women are on shaky ground, wondering what type of person to look for, what type of person to be, and how to interact with those they court. With this foundation, the adventure of courtship can be pursued with confidence, joy, and much hope in God.

Discussion Questions:

1. What are some of the pitfalls a couple might fall into if they are dating, and don't acknowledge any distinctions in masculinity and femininity? How about in marriage?

2. As a man, what traits of masculinity will you work on developing? As a woman, what traits of femininity will you embrace in a new way?

3. What did you think about the authors' assertion that a woman has power in how she responds to a man's leadership?

4. What are some ways a woman can affirm a man's leadership in a professional or academic environment? And how can a man practice leadership with women who don't have the responsibility of submitting to him?

4
Leading
and Submitting

Introduction

In Chapter 3 we laid the framework for masculinity and femininity, describing the traits that any man or woman, especially those entering their teen and adult years and beginning their search for a spouse, will want to develop as the foundation for their courtship and marriage. Now, in Chapter 4, we will examine how a maturely masculine man and a maturely feminine woman will interact with each other. And this means we must dive into a controversial subject: Leadership & Submission. Leadership between two equals is not contradictory; we see it even in the Trinity. With regard to essence, Jesus can say, "I and the Father are one" (John 10:30). With regard to function, Jesus can say, "the Father is greater than I" (John 14:28).

But many of us bristle at the notion of different roles within male/female relationships. Since the Fall of man corrupted the harmonious, complementary relationship between male and female personhood, we see many distortions of masculinity and femininity in the world around us. So it is important to distinguish mature, biblical masculinity and femininity from its cheap imitations, corrupted because of our sinful hearts. We'll do that in this chapter, show some examples, and tie this back to how it applies to people interested in marrying.

Mature Masculinity is Neither Chauvinistic Nor Passive

The biblical beauty of mature masculinity can be contrasted with the two distortions that arise, namely *machismo* and *passivity*. Passivity is by far the more significant problem in Western culture today, so I'll tackle this one first. It is also more difficult to detect; we are immune to it since it is so pervasive.

Passivity is where a guy simply gives a woman what she wants when she wants it, and fails to take initiative or assert himself so as not to be an imposition. He incorrectly assumes that by doing what she asks he is making her happy. That's how a guy thinks: "If I want something, I'll ask for it." But what a woman typically wants from a man – particularly in the area of romance – is for him to, very literally, take her up into an adventure that is larger than her own pursuits. She is not fashioned to have a man come alongside her, simply living with her and staying out of trouble. At the core of her being, she longs to see leadership she can respond to and enthusiastically support. The passive man refuses to work on the relationship itself; it is not very important to him. If it happens to go well, great – he'll enjoy it. But if it doesn't, oh well – time to invest elsewhere. This man goes with the flow; whatever happens happens.

A passive man might be embarrassed to take initiative in a relationship with a woman. He puts out "feelers" to see if she is interested in him. If he talks to her, he does so in a sort of sheepish way, always trying to protect himself from any personal exposure, as that would involve risk. So when the last semester of school comes along, and she is about to move 300 miles back to her home town or to take a job, he figures, "Oh well. I guess she must not like me, or she'd stay around." He is treating her as if she was another man. What he ought to do, both gently and courageously, is assume the risk and inform her of his interest. In effect, he needs to suggest to her that she alter her previous plan and come along with him. This requires a mature willingness on his part to assume responsibility not just for himself, but for her as well. Many men today lack such confidence. Such a man is himself confused as to who he is, so why would he want to go through life with a woman committed to him? It seems frightening. Passive men take the path of least resistance. Even if a passive man does pursue a woman, chances are he at most wants to have just his emotional and sexual desires met. He is not truly prepared to lead, protect, and provide for her in an active fashion. This is partly why the cohabitation rate is so high, and why the birth rate is so low.

Male chauvinism, on the other hand, is much more easily detected. If a man is unmarried and too macho, he will be shunned since women are averse to chauvinism. Such a man doesn't have the "nice guy" appeal of the passive man who, because he has no particular convictions, passions, or direction in life, lacks anything to avoid. The harsh man doesn't go with the flow; he forces his will upon others by sheer, unbridled strength. This is not the disposition that tends toward loving, protecting, and providing for a woman;

rather it hurts and takes advantage of a woman. There is one kind of woman this might attract, and it happens with enough frequency that it is worth noting. Some women come from broken homes where their father was emotionally and verbally (if not physically) abusive. Consequently, they want to be loved, but they have no positive standard as to how a man should treat them. Not having received a significant amount of healthy male affirmation, they may accept what appears to be love and affection from a strong man. Such a man is attractive because of his strength, and no matter how irrational it may be, in her insecurity this sort of woman will often blame herself for his expressions of harshness. She can love such a man though she has no respect for him.

These, then, are the two perversions of biblical masculinity.[1]

Mature Femininity Is Neither Obsequious Nor Domineering

Great myths abound about what the nature of a feminine disposition involves. A feminine woman in the minds of some might conjure images of

1. Given the scope of this book, I won't go into how perversions of masculinity and femininity are related to the Fall of man per Genesis 3:16. There, God spoke to the woman, "Your desire shall be for your husband, and he shall rule over you." It is not that male headship was caused by the Fall; God ordained male headship by virtue of how he created Eve for Adam. Yet the Fall results in Eve seeking to dominate her husband, and in response her husband sometimes asserts his leadership in an uncontrolled, inordinate, tyrannical fashion.

the Victorian woman, unable to perform menial tasks without her servants' help, and shrieking at the sight of a spider. We've covered most of the ground in the last chapter, so let's first touch on the error of unintelligent "obedience". Some women think they are being submissive wives as long as they tell their husband whatever he wants to hear and do whatever he asks them to do. In the realm of unmarried women, this takes the form of a woman who is willing to do anything to get a guy. As long as she has his company and the semblance of his love, she is glad to do anything that keeps him satisfied. The sort of woman who gets involved with the harsh, chauvinistic man described above often assumes this disposition of slavish devotion. Sadly, she is used to being treated like dirt, so it is no surprise for her that her boyfriend/husband would treat her the same way. Even a woman who has not been abused per se might exhibit this type of doormat behavior if her sense of self-worth is strongly linked to her relational status instead of her relationship with God. She believes the true measure of a godly, worthy woman is one who is dating or married, so she will put up with any sort of man just to guarantee her relationship status.

But a truly feminine demeanor does not prohibit acting on the occasional need to strongly disagree with a man or with one's husband. Femininity does not deny or exclude intelligence, rationality, and an ability to make a convincing argument. In a marriage relationship, a strong wife is an asset to her husband. She can give him insightful feedback, expand his horizons to matters he may not have considered, and lovingly rebuke him when he is sinning. What a godly wife aims for at such moments is an attitude that, while affirming his leadership, seeks to sharpen it. She is not seeking to take advantage of his weaknesses by usurping his leadership. Rather, she wishes to encourage, advise, correct, and rebuke to the end that his leadership might be enhanced, his effectiveness increased, his capacities enlarged. "She does him good, and not harm, all the days of her life" (Prov. 31:12). At the end of the day, such a woman can submit to her husband knowing that he ultimately bears the responsibility before God for their relationship.

The domineering woman is the usurper. Her desire is to rule over her husband or the men around her. Such a woman may get what she wants, only to be grieved by the emasculation of the men in her midst. I've heard that about 10 per cent of women propose to their husbands. Of these 10 per cent, I wonder how many wish their husbands had proposed to them. A domineering woman will often treat her husband as though she thinks he is a wimp, although she may never admit that publicly or even to herself.

A Warning and an Example

In our culture and time, the most common errors are passive men and domineering women. And the warning is that they tend to find each other! Opposites attract, as they say. The man finds a woman who will assume his responsibility of leadership for him, allowing him to continue in his comfortable prolonged adolescence, free from the risks involved with taking responsibility. She finds a man who will allow her to do what she wants to do and control the family, unhindered. And frequently these women get what they want from their man, but still are grieved.

One example of how this plays out might be a woman who wants to have family devotions and asks her husband if they can do that sometime. Nothing happens. Two weeks later on the way home from church she makes another oblique comment about how wonderful it is that the Andersons do family devotions once a week. All of a sudden he says, "That sounds fantastic! We'll start having family devotions every Monday night, starting tomorrow." So now what does she do? Chances are she'll resist his decision. Strange as it may sound for a man, it's true. She says she doesn't want to impose on his schedule, but in reality, she doesn't want him to do the family devotions because of her prompting but rather because he himself is convinced that it is good and right. So she replies, "No, that's OK, sweetheart. I know you are busy at work and you need to relax when you come home. Don't worry, I'm having a great time in the women's Bible study." Now I would suggest that she is not necessarily rejecting his leadership. She is probably just trying to ascertain if he is exercising **real** leadership. If he then caves in, it is clear that he never was serious about his decision in the first place. And if he does do it just to please her, she is grieved. If this man is foolish, he is left scratching his head and saying, "But I thought I gave her what she wanted."

This is a good summary of the principles we've been talking about. First, a man needs to lead a wife with a degree of gentle, controlled, deliberate firmness. He must not be wishy-washy. Secondly, a woman needs to let a man do the leading. He may need to take baby-steps at first. He needs to walk before he can run. When he shows the least inkling of leadership, she ought to affirm and nurture it. In the example above, it may have been wise for her to agree to his Monday night family devotion idea. Who knows, maybe he would have actually done it? And if he did, her support and enthusiastic joy would be an encouragement to him to continue on this path.

This points to an important principle. Not all men are marriage material for all women and vice versa. A strong, godly woman should not marry a man who is not able to lead her. She will be frustrated all her life and her faith will be dwarfed because he will not be able to lead her in the paths of the upright. Likewise, a man who marries a woman who is not a blessing to him will find his capabilities and influence (in his vocation, or ministry, or community) to be limited. To put it simply, he will be less effective outside his home (which is his God-given domain) if he has to spend all his time maintaining his home (which should be his wife's domain).

A Word to Those Not Yet Married

I realize much of this seems more applicable to married folk. But there are two key points that the unmarried can take to heart.

First, cultivate the habits of mature masculinity or femininity. To unmarried men, the lesson is to apply and cultivate a manhood that doesn't err on the side of passivity or chauvinism. Young women, take heed as to how you treat the men in your midst. The habits you form here will be with you all your life and will surely impact how you treat your husband. Do you find yourself immediately critical of the decisions that men make? Such a habit in marriage can easily breed a passive husband - one who prefers peace and quiet rather than the criticism and attack that inevitably accompany his attempts at leadership.

And while you are at it, take notice of those around you. That is why the teenage years are so important. As boys and girls become sexual adults at puberty, they begin to be attracted to the opposite sex. The question is: What kind of traits do they look for and admire?

Young women, the young men who are exhibiting the sort of mature masculinity we've been describing are the ones you should be more eager to affirm, receive strength from, and nurture. "Let no one despise you for your youth, but set the believers an example in speech, in conduct, in love, in faith, in purity" (1 Tim. 4:12). Is this what you look for in a man? One who sets a godly example for others?

Likewise, young men, consider the ladies in your midst. Look to the inner beauty of a quiet disposition that stems from security in God and an ability to give of herself in such a way that makes you stronger and more effective. That is the sort of woman to pursue – don't let her get away! "Charm is deceitful, and beauty is vain, but a woman who fears the Lord is to be praised" (Prov. 31:30). Is this what you look for in a woman?

What Does All this Mean for an Unmarried Man and Woman in a Courtship Situation?

So let's take this to where the rubber meets the road. In what manner should two 20-year-olds become acquainted with each other? Practically, things pertaining to your interaction may look different depending on the culture in which you find yourselves. The Bible gives us principles and then we need to use our judgment to implement them with methods that seem most appropriate for our unique set of circumstances.

As a young man, be watching her behavior, attitude, and demeanor to see if you find the responsive, affirming, life-giving companionship that will help you in your calling and service to God. As a young woman, watch him to see if you find in his behavior gentle, self-sacrificial, bold, God-centered, Christ-following leadership that you can joyfully submit to and that will give you a solid framework in which to manifest the gifts God has given you.

As an unmarried man, practice and clothe yourself in your leadership role in this situation by paying for her when the two of you participate together in activities alone or with others. Set the tone of your interactions in terms of conversation topics, level of depth, and appropriate use of humor. You might also display gestures of honor like holding the door open for her, and setting boundaries with regard to how you display affection. In short, begin to demonstrate (albeit in nascent form) something of what you will demonstrate as a husband. These behavioral patterns will inevitably be the outworking of what you are internally. A woman looking out for these character traits will see you as you really are.

It's true that an unmarried woman does not owe submission to a man she's not married to; the Bible tells a woman to be submissive to her own husband, not to men in general. So don't blindly and irresponsibly "submit" if your boyfriend tells you how to invest your money or leads you into sexual sin. However, your demeanor with men should encourage them to continually become worthier of receiving submission. In fact, during even the initial stages of a relationship you can practice leading and joyful submission in ways appropriate to the limited level of commitment of this season of your relationship. A woman can joyfully affirm a man's leadership as he takes initiative and plans an activity for the two of them, for example, and by allowing him to take the initiative and set the pace and tone of the relationship.

How About a Casual Friendship with a Fellow Christian at Church?

Here a man cannot initiate the kinds of discussions that he might with his wife, or even with his girlfriend. Nevertheless, he bears the primary responsibility to build protections against the development of any kind of inappropriate intimacy. This applies whether or not either of them is married. If the relationship is "just friendship", he needs to honor that and treat her appropriately. If she is unmarried and a Christian, and he becomes romantically interested, he needs to explicitly inform her of that rather than merely changing his behavior and assuming she will join him emotionally. A respectable man will make his intentions clear and not play games with a woman.

Or Perhaps with a Coworker?

In the case of a totally platonic, professional relationship, masculinity and femininity can still be honored. Even with a female superior, a man can seek to honor her femininity in culturally appropriate ways. He could open the door, offer his chair, and speak in a voice that is quieter and gentler. He can give particular attention when listening to her. Men, who are generally more task-oriented than women, are typically less prone to feel a sense of rudeness if a man interrupts or skips the small talk. The other man has saved him the time and hassle of speaking (the purpose of the conversation, after all, was probably to accomplish something). On the contrary, when women speak, they generally want not only to relate information (and complete a task), they are also attempting to bond relationally. A man who is sensitive to this is honoring the femininity of his coworker and not trampling upon it. And a Christian woman can honor the masculinity of her coworkers by affirming their leadership, by praising their accomplishments, and by being appreciative of the contributions and assistance they provide.

Conclusions

So no matter what life stage you are in, now is the time to develop mature masculinity or femininity, and to encourage the traits with the men and women in your family, church, workplace, anywhere. If you are seeking a spouse, look for these characteristics in those you consider for marriage. Seek out someone who will joyfully affirm your leadership as a man, or who will tenderly, responsibly lead you if you are a woman.

When you find this person, how should you proceed to cultivate your relationship? We'll explore that next. But the practical tips to follow are based on a strong commitment to and practice of godly, mature masculinity and femininity.

Discussion Questions:

1. Before reading this chapter, what did you think about women submitting to men? Did this chapter change your understanding in any way?

2. Where do you fall on the "Passivity/Machismo" spectrum of men or the "Doormat/Domineering" spectrum for women?

3. As a woman, how do you react when a man takes initiative or leadership? Do you appreciate it or reject it?

4. What risks are involved for a man to assume leadership or for a woman to wait to respond? What role does trust in God play in the development of these traits?

5. How can you cultivate leadership and submissiveness right now, whether you are married or single?

5
Choosing Wisely

Introduction

Now that we've laid the foundation of understanding the nature of the partners, we're ready to tackle the formation of the partnership itself. You might want to sit down and write your list of what you are looking for in a spouse. This is not a waste of time in fantasyland; this is a crucial part of the process to both intentionally and prayerfully think about the kind of person you want to marry and the kind of person you want to become. Next ask yourself if you are in the process of becoming the sort of person that such a person would want to marry. In other words, are you becoming the sort of person that would attract the kind of person that you want to be with? It is far easier to point out faults in the lives of others than to soberly examine yourself, and to maintain a teachable spirit before the Lord. Yet you will find marriage to be more like a school of sanctification than a neverending holiday at the beach. A humble spirit that seeks first to admit wrong rather than to accuse the other can contribute as much or more to a successful marriage than your choice of partner. Yet there is no reason to choose a bad partner, either. And it is to that subject that we now turn.

It is possible to err either by setting standards that are too high or ones that are too low. As you develop your list of what you are looking for, talk it over with your parents, friends, and counselors to make sure your list is both rigorous and realistic.

In the following section, I'm going to address young men and women separately. But this doesn't mean that the men should skip the section addressed to women or that the women should skip the section addressed to men. Rather, men and women should seek to learn from both sections, as we're talking about both *becoming* (a godly spouse) and *recognizing* (a godly spouse).[1]

---

1. I am indebted to Rick Holland for this concept of "becoming" and "recognizing". Pastor Rick Holland of Grace Community Church in Sun Valley, CA gave an excellent series on Relationships in 1999, all of which can be found (MP3 format) online: http://www.crossroadsministry.net/crossroads/mp3.asp?dlyear=1999. I understand he is writing a book based on these messages, but I have not yet seen the manuscript at the time of this writing.

The Choice of a Wife
<u>Objective Criteria</u>

1. Is she a Christian?

It is clear that the Bible calls us to only marry a Christian (2 Cor. 6:14-18).[2] If we are only to marry in the Lord, it is equally clear that we ought only to court (or date) a woman *who is in the Lord*. This is the case because the purpose of the courting process is, with prayer, to carefully consider the possibility of marriage. It is also true because getting our emotions entangled with an unbeliever tends to turn even strong, earnest Christians away from the Lord (1 Kgs. 11:1-8).

2. Does she evidence some degree of maturity?

Does she have godly companions? Are they the kind that encourage her to focus merely on shallow aspects of life like beauty and clothes and reading *Cosmopolitan*? Do they belittle her aspirations to be a wife and mother and insist she focus on her career? Do they encourage her in her walk with God?

Does she have a servant's heart? Is there a track record of faithfulness? Does she pursue God in a corporate community? Is she teachable? To these,

2. See, for example, *Whom Shall I Marry?* by Andrew Swanson, Banner of Truth, 1996.

we might add: Does she have a nurturing disposition or is she self-absorbed? Women tend to be more relational, so they often are more immediately expressive in conversation. Does she talk mainly about herself and seek to draw attention? Does she love children? If she never wants to have children, this should be examined. More often than not, married Christians have selfish reasons for remaining childless. But a woman in particular should have a high view of motherhood. She should consider such a vocation an honor, and not have accepted worldly notions that disparage pouring out one's life for the next generation.[3] Given that a woman in marriage comes alongside a man to assist him in his calling, and to complete him, another set of questions is pertinent. Does she feel that her career should take an equal or greater priority to his? Is she willing to help him in his career and ministry callings? Will she submit to his leadership, and is she demonstrating this now in ways appropriate to the stage of the relationship?

A cautionary note on flirtation seems warranted. Female flirtation is often based on immaturity. By

3. A woman does not need to be married to have this orientation. Indeed, all women should develop a desire to invest their lives in the eternal well-being of others. This may or may not include motherhood (though it often will). Noel Piper has just published a helpful book in this regard entitled *Faithful Women and Their Extraordinary God* (Crossway, 2005). Mrs. Piper highlights the life and ministry of five women (Sarah Edwards, Lilias Trotter, Gladys Aylward, Esther Ahn Kim, and Helen Roseveare) and shows how they poured out their lives for the sake of the eternal happiness of others. Of these five, only Edwards was married.

this I mean that she has no true interest – she just wants her ego stroked by getting men to pay attention to her. Such a woman is deriving her sense of worth by whether or not men are paying attention to her. This is also why some women dress suggestively.[4]

Subjective Criteria

Having considered objective criteria, let's now consider a few areas of subjective criteria. Some of you may be saying: "Why? If she meets the biblical requirements for a good wife, what else is there to consider?" Well, meeting objective criteria is certainly a good thing, but as we'll see, subjective criteria prove to be equally important. The biblical commands to husband and wife are difficult to fulfill. Consequently, it simply makes good sense to marry someone that isn't merely a good person, but whom you also get along well with. Secondly, subjective criteria are important because God made us both rational and emotional beings. Our minds and our hearts are more intertwined than we often realize. When we're commanded in the Scriptures to love our wives or

4. It is possible that such women are not being given a proper amount of healthy male affection in their homes. They need strong, male affirmation. The trouble is if they do not get it at home, they often seek it in boyfriends (and might be willing to sleep with them to get it), and yet the men they attract are the selfish kind who will use them and hurt them.

respect our husbands, it ought to be understood that God is not after some mere robotic obedience without the involvement of the heart's affections. God wants our hearts to be involved, and it is for our good that they work in concert with our mind.[5]

1. Am I physically attracted to her?

I tread lightly here, knowing that I'm probably stepping on a few toes. I think we need to be honest: the Bible celebrates physical attraction in marriage. Song of Solomon captures with vivid language the delight of marital love, including physical attraction (Song 1:10-11; 4:1-5, 7). Let's not be more spiritual than God is. While our world may idolize youth and physical beauty, that doesn't mean that we as Christians should go to the opposite extreme and say that physical attractiveness has no significance. God is the one who wired us so that physical attraction is sexually stimulating. But while physical attraction should be present to some degree, it should by no means be the only (or even primary) basis for choosing a partner.[6]

5. All obedience to God should be the overflow of heartfelt affections – for this is in fact part of what God commands.

6. And the degree of attractiveness should increase during the relationship; it is healthy if the other person becomes more beautiful the more one knows them. It is also wise, after marriage, to choose to find your spouse physically attractive, by ignoring their less attractive traits and focusing on what you find most desirable.

2. Do we share intellectual synergy?

A man will probably find it difficult to lead a woman who is more intellectually capable, creative, and resourceful than he is. Important sidebar: men tend to thrive when they feel needed. A man married to a woman who is clearly his superior will either try to lead the family and be frustrated (perhaps even devastated) at his sense of inadequacy, try to stifle her gifts by being domineering and abusive, or (more likely) he will just check out (mentally and spiritually) and let her take care of everything. Regardless, his response will almost certainly not be healthy for their family.

To avoid misunderstanding, please note that intellectual capability is not necessarily measured by one's educational level. A man may have had more formal education to fulfill his chosen profession, but that doesn't mean his intellectual capabilities necessarily exceed those of a woman who did not obtain as much formal education. Rather, synergy with respect to intellectual capability can be gauged by mutual choice of conversation topics, an ability or inclination to dive into complicated subjects and try to make sense out of them, a desire to keep growing intellectually throughout one's lifetime (or not), and whether one prefers numerous hours watching television or reading high-quality literature.[7]

3. Do I enjoy her company?

The last subjective criterion I wish to mention is both a collective and a foundational consideration: Do you enjoy her company? The woman can be of remarkable quality and highly endorsed by your pastor, parents, and friends, but if you simply don't enjoy being with her, this will make things unnecessarily difficult. You should like her, and like being with her. I am emphatically not arguing for a secular notion of "compatibility" that says you have to come hatched out of the same mold. Two very different people can have a wonderful marriage, but there ought to be an enjoyment present in your interactions.

The Choice of a Husband

Objective Criteria

1. Is he a Christian?

To reiterate, it is clear that the Bible calls us to only marry a Christian (2 Cor. 6:14-18). This means

---

7. This matter, however, is not entirely morally neutral. The fact that God has communicated to us through a Book does say something significant about the importance of good reading skills. Further, part of the great commandment is that we love the Lord our God with all our minds. Thoughtful reading and thinking, then, are essential to the Christian life.

turning down an unbeliever even if he's just asking you out for a cup of coffee. Because women are more relationally oriented, it's important to guard your heart before understanding where a man is in his walk with God. While there are some success stories of "missionary dating", it is wise to let a man grow in his faith outside of a romantic relationship. Men are interested in the conquest, and many will do whatever it takes even to falsely convince a woman that he is a Christian. Remember too that a woman is called to submit to her husband. It is nearly impossible for even a strong Christian woman to maintain and grow in her faith while following an unbeliever.

2. Does he evidence some degree of maturity?

Give particular attention to evaluating the degree of self-control men exhibit. In Titus chapter 2, Paul tells Titus (a young pastor) to "urge the younger men to be self-controlled" (Titus 2:6). Young men have a tendency to possess a large degree of pent-up energy and zeal. These can be wonderful assets if directed in a God-honoring direction. And they are terrible liabilities if directed elsewhere. So questions like the following are relevant: Does he control his temper (anger)? Does he control his speech? A lack of control in speech can include the use of crude language or inappropriate humor, speaking harshly in anger, or making commitments and failing to keep them. Psalm 15 describes one who walks blamelessly, in part, as one who "swears to his own hurt and does not change" (Ps. 15:4). I think this refers to "letting your 'yes' be 'yes' and your 'no' be 'no'", as Jesus said (Matt. 5:37).

In contrast, many men are sadly passive, failing to take initiative or leadership. Again, it can be very difficult for a woman to follow and submit to a man who refuses to lead. If he isn't sure what he wants to do with his life, if he takes an inordinately long time advancing your relationship, if all his free time is spent in front of the television, consider whether he is ready to lead you and your family.

Another area that can be revelatory is a man's approach to his work. Does he show up on time? Does he only work hard when others are watching? Or does he work so hard it's at the expense of church attendance and regular time in the Word? In his private life, does he evidence good priorities by what he chooses to do and what he chooses not to do? Does he demonstrate that he has clear ethical and spiritual convictions?

The type of person a man chooses as his closest associates is indicative of the man's maturity level. Does he choose godly companions? Do he and his friends have servants' hearts? Are they faithful men? Do they regularly attend church and demonstrate that following God in the corporate community of believers is a priority? Or do they spend more time playing video games than sharpening and encouraging each other in their faith? Are they teachable and open to correction, or are they stiff-necked and proud?

Women need to watch for flirtatious men as well. Flirtation on the part of a guy is generally either an expression of passivity (able to "initiate", but not able to take responsibility and leadership), fear (truly wanting a relationship but lacking the courage to take the risk), or immaturity. It can be easy for a guy to show attention to a pretty girl, but far more difficult for that man to implement a plan to get to know that woman better in a God-honoring way to see if they ought to be married. Responsibility and leadership demand a higher price than the mere display of interest called "initiation". When flirtation is motivated by fear, he may truly have a plan to pursue the woman in a God-honoring manner; he simply fears rejection, so he beats around the bush rather than getting to the punch line. The immature man has no true interest whatsoever; he just wants his ego stroked by causing a woman to pay attention to him. Or he may simply want physical intimacy (sex or foreplay) without marital commitment.

Subjective Criteria

Women, too, need to consider subjective criteria in evaluating a husband. Having a husband she finds attractive and fun to be with can make it much easier to submit to and be faithful to him.

1. Do I find him physically attractive?

Physical attraction is more important for visually oriented men. It is sometimes noted that women care less about what a man looks like, and more about how a man treats her. However, this too has limits. The woman in Song of Solomon also praises her lover's appearance (Song 5:10-16). A woman should not marry a man she finds repulsive or that she is not physically attracted to at all. Many women will find that though they are eager for sex before marriage, after a hard day, with her kids wearing her out, she will find many times when she is less inclined to make love than her husband is. Physical attraction to her husband can certainly help. But, as with men, women should not value physical attraction too highly. And many women say that they find their partner becomes more physically attractive as his other objective and subjective qualities become dearer to her.

2. Do we share intellectual synergy?

A woman should recognize that she would have to submit to this man. This will likely prove more difficult for her if she is two or three times more intellectually capable, creative, and resourceful than he is. If she marries such a man, she may find herself downplaying her own strengths in order to avoid embarrassing her spouse. But it is wise to not be too black and white in this area. It is altogether plausible that a female doctor might marry a blue-collar worker who is a brilliant self-taught philosopher and theologian. His leadership can also grow as he gains experience in marriage. Conversely, a woman should be careful about marrying a man who intimidates her and makes her feel foolish because of his greater knowledge and education. But again, if he is patient with her and is stimulated by her other qualities, this may not be a showstopper.

3. Do I enjoy his company?

The man is tall, dark, and handsome, a strong, godly leader, and we have all the same goals and passions. He's Mr. Right, right? Not necessarily! If you're bored out of your mind talking with him, if your sense of humor doesn't click with his, if you don't enjoy any of the same activities, or if you run out of things to talk about after "hi, how was your day?", think twice. Marriage lasts a lifetime and you will spend plenty of it outside the bedroom, outside the church sanctuary, and without discussing how many kids to have. Make sure the time you spend together going grocery shopping, spending a free Saturday together, or talking over a cup of coffee is time you both delight in and treasure.

Let's now turn to some dangers that men and women face in the premarital relationship process itself.

Dangers Men and Women Face in the Premarital Relationship Process

Underestimating Cultural Differences

I want to avoid the danger of the legalism involved in forbidding such relationships (e.g. interracial marriage), but also acknowledge that there may be issues stemming from different family or cultural backgrounds that would require discussion. For example, expectations with regard to child-raising. Does one partner come from a tradition that sees the first five years of a child's life as the time to push him or her as hard as possible to ensure they will become an Olympic athlete or world-famous pianist? How will Christmas be celebrated? Halloween? Do the man and woman have similar expectations as to how often the extended families should be visited? Does she intend to serve as a missionary doctor in a village in Uganda her entire life, while he is absolutely committed to climbing the corporate ladder in London?

Women's Attire

A safe guideline is that a man should give care to where his eyes go, and a woman should give care to the way she dresses.[8] A man's eyes generally go to a woman's clothing line. Tight clothing accentuates a woman's physical features. An attractive woman who dresses provocatively will easily elicit the attention of men. But often she thereby attracts the wrong kind of men: either non-Christians or relatively weak, lustful Christians. Conversely, an attractive woman who dresses modestly will keep the majority of undesirable men at bay. Dressing provocatively and attractively is easy. Dressing modestly and unattractively is also easy (and neither more godly nor more spiritual!). It is an art form – and rare – for a woman to dress *both modestly and attractively*. A woman who does this is a gem!

There are two principles at work here:

8. Nowadays the opposite of that statement would also apply, but to a lesser extent. Statistically speaking, men and women alike are more fascinated with the beauty of women than that of men.

1. Men are generally more visually oriented than women. This is not inherently sinful; God made them that way. This originates in how their hormones are activated. Though a man's visual orientation is not inherently sinful, it poses dangers both for men and women. A man should take care to guard his eyes, as Job pledged to do (Job 31:1). A woman should not dress provocatively so as to get attention from men. *Whereas a man often lusts by looking, a woman can exhibit lust by her desire to be looked upon*. Such a woman should mortify this lust. In addition to dishonoring God through such selfish expression, she will only make her life miserable by attracting the wrong kind of guys, and by misdirecting her energy at the expense of developing more important qualities. Which brings me to the second principle:

2. This one is subtler, and women often don't realize it. A scantily dressed woman may receive significant attention from a man, *until another such woman comes along*. If his attraction for her is shallow, neither will it be stable nor long lasting. And no matter how beautiful or beautifully attired a woman is, it is just a matter of time until someone comes along and outshines her. A woman should be careful not to become involved with a man who only desires her physically, or she

may quickly lose him when he loses that sense of thrill or conquest.

Uneven Pace of Relationship

Men tend to value that which is attained with great effort. A woman whose affections are easily won is often less prized. A woman should therefore guard her emotions by modest speech as well as her physical appearance through modest dress. In relationships, women tend to move faster emotionally than men do. They more readily give their hearts away. They often do this either by sharing too much about themselves, or by encouraging or allowing the man to share too much of himself. A man should exhibit a pattern of leadership in conversation to avoid her having to bear the responsibility of playing captain.[9] Women should take pains to guard their heart; they should give it away only to the right kind of man, who earns it, and only after he has given her his heart. In other words, she should be letting him set the emotional pace of the relationship. If he is incapable as a leader, and she is not willing to respect him in this capacity,

9. Incidentally, one of the reasons women have a hard time stopping communication processes in which the man is sharing too much – one of the reasons women in general, to be quite frank, have a more difficult time saying no – is that they are created by God to be responders. They more naturally want to please others and thus be loved by them. When the network of people to whom they are emotionally related are all happy with them, it is then that they themselves are most happy.

there is a reasonable doubt about their marriage prospects.

The same is true in regards to the physical pace of relationship; men tend to value that which is attained with great effort. Both partners must be equally vigilant to slow the physical progression of the relationship; this burden should not be borne by the woman alone. While emotional progress is necessary for the progress of the relationship towards marriage, physical progress is not. Physical intimacy (foreplay) should be reserved for marriage; both foreplay and the sex act belong to the marriage bed (Heb. 13:4).

Failing to Consider the Whole Person

Different types of Christians are more susceptible to different types of errors. *Exclusive* consideration of either objective criteria or subjective criteria can lead to problems. Analytical men raised in strong churches often give too much emphasis to objective criteria – they are simply looking for someone who satisfies a checklist. Women from broken homes needy for male affection sometimes give too much emphasis to subjective criteria – settling for anyone they enjoy being with **at the time** without due consideration for the future; enjoying the affection he gives her at the moment, without considering if he would be a good father for her children. Either extreme can lead to problems.

Getting Hung Up on the Past

One final danger of which you should beware: do not overly consider the person's past sins. Such shortsightedness fails to take God's grace into account. Failure in one's past can often be a prerequisite for success in the future because God draws people to himself by bringing them to the end of self-dependency. All of us have scars and sins. One should consider not so much where a person has been as where they are going – is there evidence of a trajectory towards increasing holiness in the person's life, a Godward orientation? It's true that a baby Christian would often do better growing in his or her walk with the Lord first rather than immediately becoming involved in a romantic relationship; there is a concept of "foundational" maturity, if you will. But I also recognize that sometimes God brings along a person – perhaps someone previously involved in the new believer's life – who becomes both an agent of sanctification, and, in God's timing, a life partner in marriage. It often happens with great results. But I give an extra warning to women considering marriage to a man who is less spiritually mature than she is. In an effort to follow and submit to her husband, she may be tempted to smother her own growth. Each case should be considered carefully by asking questions such as: *Is this potential romantic partner encouraging or discouraging Christian growth in the life of the other?*

In the next chapter, we'll discuss stages of relationships, and a natural, healthy progression of a premarital romance.

Discussion Questions:

1. Have you ever before made a list of what you are looking for in a spouse? If not, why not? Take a few minutes right now, and brainstorm some ideas for what might go on a list like this. Share them in the group.

2. Were you surprised by the encouragement to include physical attraction as a selection criteria? Do you think you give this too much weight, or pay too little attention to this?

3. The author asserts that women should dress both modestly and attractively. Is this common in your community? What side do you tend to err on?

4. <u>For the women</u>: Do you find that in the past you have given your heart too readily? How can you slow this process?

5. <u>For the men</u>: How can you be protective of a woman in this area, while still pursuing her?

6. Does your boyfriend/girlfriend meet the criteria laid out in this chapter? Are you and your partner encouraging or discouraging Christian growth in the life of the other?

6
Proceeding Carefully

Let's discuss the progression of a premarital relationship in terms of four stages. The first is "Friendship and Initiation". This is the beginning point at which two people are getting to know each other, but without any commitment or exclusivity. The second stage, "The Beginnings of Romantic Involvement", is taking the relationship to the next level. Many would call this phase "Defining the Relationship". There is articulation of intentions and exclusivity begins. "Later Stages of a Romantic Relationship" is similar to step 2, but with enhanced levels of intimacy and intentionality. And then the last stage we'll look at is "Leaving and Cleaving", exploring some of the warnings and activities appropriate to engagement.

1. Friendship and Initiation

The first stage is a friendship. A strong friendship forms the foundation for everything that follows. In the stage of friendship, it is anticipated that men and women would seek to enjoy being in the company of one another, without any sense of exclusivity (i.e. they are not "together" or "with" each other). Consequently, there is no romantic interaction at this time, but instead a great opportunity to learn about the values, family life, and pursuits of each other.

I realize many of you reading this book in the United Kingdom and Australia have less of a distinctively Christian subculture than is available in the United States. Perhaps an advantage of this is that it forces your life of faith to be genuine, lived from the inside out, rather than from mere external conformity. In a "Christian bubble" it can be easy to say or do certain things to look like a "good Christian" without actually being one. God indeed calls us *individually* as sinners to repent of our rebellion, and to submit and embrace Christ as Savior and Lord, treasuring Him above all things.

There must be an internal reality to our faith, or we're not truly born again. Though God indeed calls *individuals* to Himself, he does not do it in isolation to others. He simultaneously calls each person into a community with others whom He has likewise called; this is the essence of the "church". Wherever Christians live, they are called to be a new community – a community of the "called-out ones" – a church. Therefore it is important to value Christian community, recognizing that if we've responded to Christ's call, we will naturally see fellow Christians as our true family members and cultivate a special love for them (Gal. 6:10; John 15:12; I John 3:14). So pursue cultivating deep bonds with fellow Christians out of love for God. A by-product of being in relationship with other Christians will be that God will open your eyes to the sort of person with whom you can build an even more special lifelong commitment (marriage).

Suppose you have Christian friends through your church and larger Christian network and there is someone in particular that strikes your fancy. Make this a source of prayer, while also (to the degree possible) seeking advice from more mature Christians about the quality of this other person.

If one or both individuals are not of an age that they could marry (15–18-year-olds) in the foreseeable future, the relationship should not extend beyond this initial stage of friendship. The purpose of a premarital relationship is, as we have previously established, to pursue marriage. Even if you discovered that the two of you did want to get married, the need to wait several years might prove quite onerous. In most cases, teens today do not date with marriage in mind, but for physical and emotional closeness, from peer pressure, or from a sense that having a boyfriend or girlfriend is necessary for significance. As we've mentioned, none of these reasons are acceptable for a close, exclusive relationship and all of them are a form of using others. It is right for teenagers as well to have a sense of purpose in their actions and a respect for members of the opposite sex.

But at the same time I would not want to rule out the possibility of God opening your eyes to your future spouse during the teen years, as that would seem to inappropriately limit God. I do think it is especially rare in our day given the prevailing tendency of immaturity, but your teenage years are not inherently required to be a period of wandering. Teens can (and should) be raised by parents and pastors to embrace God as their treasure (Matt. 13:44) and consequently to accept their call to maturely express their masculinity and femininity as singles, recognizing that God has wired most of them for a future marriage. Paul's advice to Timothy comes to mind: "Let no one despise you for your youth, but set the believers an example in speech, in conduct, in love, in faith, in purity" (1 Tim. 4:12). A relationship among teens would need to look different, though, from a relationship between 23-year-olds. For one, teens are generally still finding out how they are wired and where they are headed as adults. So I'd imagine 95 per cent of the interactions occurring in group settings with emotions held at bay. The relationship should be non-exclusive, avoiding discussions that nurture feelings and hopes for a shared future. Rather, each sees the other as belonging wholly to God. Things should only get serious if the two are in a position to get married within the next eighteen months or so, otherwise the exposure to sexual temptation can be too great.

But assuming both individuals are of an age that marriage in the foreseeable future is a possibility, there is a greater sense of liberty to proceed.[1]

1. Maturity is still important, mind you. I am not saying that age can substitute for maturity. Immature 25-year-olds can still make a mess out of things, which is why it is so important they ought to regularly read books like Proverbs and (in the case of women) Esther and Ruth. They need to give emphasis to spiritual maturity in a context that holds marriage in high esteem. Marriage, then, will follow in due course, being neither rushed nor unduly delayed.

But what does "in the foreseeable future" mean? Many people naturally wonder if there is some magic age. As I learned from Dr. Al Mohler, it makes the most sense to think of it in a simple manner: marriage equals adulthood (except where there's a gifting for singleness). This serves to discourage pursuit of marriage at the low end of the age spectrum and to encourage marriage from the time at which a young man or woman is able to be gainfully employed and consequently self-supporting. Speaking personally, I hope to raise my children in such a way that they are able to marry in their early twenties because, given our Western society of today, that is the earliest that they can be ready to take on the financial burdens of marriage and family. A previous chapter discussed some of the benefits of marrying at an early adult age. Another benefit is that they are able to grow *together* in their early adult years, increasingly understanding who they are as individuals in relation to their life partner. It only makes growing together harder to do, and the difficulties of marriage even greater, if singles already have entrenched habits, strong stylistic preferences, and an ingrained adult lifestyle that each brings into the marriage (not to mention that each already has a house full of furniture!). Under God, the identity of the (already) adult man and the woman ought to be shaped in the context of the other. This, too, is why marriage is so valuable; it is not just about sexual fulfillment. It is worth noting here because our culture values independence so highly that many young people think they need to be single and free for many years to "discover who they are". Well, certainly singleness has advantages for Christian service and the ability to give yourself entirely to the Lord and thus profit immensely in the way of Christian maturity. But even for singles such growth should invariably come in the context of intentional, authentic Christian community. So you might think of marriage as the ultimate, and most intimate, community of two. Marriage provides the sort of intimacy that results in learning things about yourself (mostly your sinfulness) that were either previously unseen or not dealt with to the degree that marriage inherently requires. It is also important that the two individuals are clearly moving in the direction of greater spiritual maturity, because simply getting into a dating relationship won't correct a misguided heart. God must be the first love of each.

Yet the initiation – that is, the pattern of leadership right from the start – needs to come from the man[2] because of the nature of masculinity and femininity. If she leads, then the relationship is distorted from day one. So the man initiates, and the woman responds. And it makes the most sense if both do their part in the context of a relational Christian community. It is helpful if parents are involved as well, but the extent of their involvement will naturally vary given the age of the man and woman, where the parents are geographically relative to the couple, and the extent to which the parents are caring and wise. Pastors or more mature couples in the church can act as wonderful surrogates when the parents aren't equipped to serve in this capacity.

As we're talking about initiation in the context of community, a cautionary note must be made. Sometimes overprotective parents reject a suitor/potential sweetheart due to personal prejudice (race, socioeconomic status, history, divorced parents, etc.). Such parents (or, by extension, youth pastors) ought to remember that the young man or young woman's testimony does not need to exactly match yours in order to be valid. What matters is that God has received him (Rom. 15:7), and that he or she is seeking to glorify God. Par-

2. Sometimes well-meaning Christians will bring up the example of Ruth as an exception (Ruth 3:9). It is important to note that Ruth was acting under the guidance of Naomi, the mother of her deceased first husband. Furthermore, laws regarding kinsmen redeemers are part of a law-covenant system that Christ has fulfilled.

ents can be motivated by selfishness, wanting to keep their kids from growing up for as long as possible (under the guise of "godly protection"). Such actions, ironically, often delay marriage unnecessarily, which in turn increases the likelihood for immorality and/or premarital strife. Alternatively, parents and spouse-seekers alike may have unbiblical, idealistic standards they hold out for a potential spouse – like prestigious, high-paying careers. It is important to emphasize that marriage is primarily to be directed to the glory of God, and if people don't treasure Him, then their marriages will be based on whatever idols are set up in His place.

2. The Beginnings of Romantic Involvement[3]

Once a man, guided by his parents and/or church community, has decided he is ready to pursue marriage and he has begun to build a friendship with a woman who seems to have the qualities of an excellent wife, it is time for him to lead the relationship to the next stage.

So what defines this next stage? Or what differentiates it from other relationships each

3. For the discussion of romantic relationships in terms of stages with subheadings of time spent, topics discussed, emotional intimacy, and accountability, I lean substantially on material developed by William Scott Croft of Capitol Hill Baptist Church. This material is online and is titled: "Courtship and Dating" CORE Seminar Curriculum (http://www.capitalhillbaptist.org). That said, one should not infer that Mr. Croft necessarily holds to all that I say here.

will inevitably have (and continue to have) with members of the opposite sex? The relationship initiated should be *exclusive, marriage-oriented,* and *principled*. By "exclusive", I mean that neither party will be romantically involved or considering romantic involvement with other people. The relationship is "marriage-oriented", in that each is actively evaluating the other as a potential spouse; he is considering whether he will ask her to marry him, and she is considering her response to that question should it be asked. While many of the qualifications (e.g. the fruits of the Spirit) will be nonnegotiable for both, there is an over-arching difference to what they are evaluating. He is seeking a helper with respect to his calling, and she is determining whether she wants to love, respect, and submit to this man, coming alongside him to assist him in his calling. It is not that her gifts and skills would not be needed or valued in such an arrangement; it is simply that his trajectory in life will shape the tone and scope of their use. Finally, by "principled" I mean that each party maintains a focus on God above all else, a desire to joyfully obey God as He's revealed himself in His Word, a commitment to seek not only his own interests, but also the interests of the other (Phil. 2:3), an embrace of the local church as God's means for Christian growth, and (last but not least) a commitment to guard the sacredness of sex.[4]

So how should the man initiate this stage of the relationship? Here it is important that the man take into account both his own and the woman's constitution, as well as any "baggage" that each may be bringing into the relationship. He should be explicit and tell her (not assuming that she's guessing it by his behavior) that he'd like the relationship to be exclusive, marriage-oriented, and principled. But he should do so in such a manner (tone of voice, body language) that, as far as it lies within his power, the conversation does not provoke an unnecessarily strong, purely emotional response on her part. He is not proposing marriage at this point! And the two are embarking on a serious, thoughtful, objective evaluation of each other. Talking too much about, "I'm trying to see if marriage is right for us" may result in her either fleeing from him in fear or losing sleep choosing her bridesmaids and the style of her wedding gown. Generally, women's hearts are more promptly engaged in the relationship (as God has constituted them to be responders). So whereas the man might not be too "emotionally involved" at this point, once he

4. See Chapter 2 of *Boy Meets Girl* by Joshua Harris (Multnomah, 2000).

has expressed his interest in her, if she shares this interest the chances are that her emotions are involved. He can moderate this effect, and so allow her to continue to appropriately evaluate both him and the relationship, by the words he chooses and in his sensitivity to her particular disposition. He should also express caution should he approach her father at this time; some women will equate this with a marriage proposal, while others feel it is a necessary prerequisite to enter this exclusive, but pre-engagement phase of the relationship.

Since it is so easy for the message to be misinterpreted, a man should not initiate this conversation if he is not yet ready to enter an exclusive, marriage-oriented, principled relationship with the woman. And if he is not ready to enter such a relationship, he ought not to single her out with overly friendly behavior and attention, as that would be deceptive and potentially manipulative. Often a man will do this in an attempt to get her to reveal her level of interest before he takes a chance and tells her what he's thinking. It is common for men to wait too long to have this conversation. They do so either because they are nervous and scared, or because they want to keep their options open. The latter is not to be a problem as long as he is careful to avoid sending signals by treating a particular woman in a preferential manner. The reality is that women often make it easy for men to move to the next stage in a relationship without any risk or leadership by revealing how they feel before he has actually disclosed his intentions. This should be avoided, as it teaches the man that he does not need to be the risk-taking, initiating leader that God has called him to be, and it can cause him to take the woman for granted.

The amount of time the man and woman spend alone at this stage should be indicative of the level of seriousness present in the relationship and the amount of time since the relationship's initiation. They should also take their age and maturity into account. In short, it is not the time for significant intimacy. Each should be trying to determine if there is a desire to get more serious. This means **not** spending three evenings a week together, but, as much as possible – and the man should look for creative ways if necessary to MAKE it possible – spending time in group settings, which naturally slow the pace of intimacy. This can be done with families, church friends, and coworkers, or through mutual involvement in various ministries (e.g. hospitality, outreach at a nursing home). This doesn't mean you can never talk alone – having coffee or lunch together occasionally can be helpful – but realize that the main danger is doing too much too soon.

Now is not the time to pour out the "juicy details" of your testimony. Guys, you need to remember that emotional guardedness is generally more difficult for women than it is for men. Women bond by sharing their feelings, desires, and their deepest, most-emotionally charged experiences. Less commonly do men realize that women can also bond when *men* share the same. So it is helpful to not make the other person an immediate confidante in deeply personal, emotional matters. Praying together can also breed excessive intimacy prematurely. Short prayer times for guidance and wisdom in the relationship in the presence of couples serving as mentors can be appropriate. The constitution, or level of emotional vulnerability, of the individuals should also be taken into account.

In the beginnings of a romantic consideration process, men and women should talk about their faith in more general terms or along the lines of contemporary or historical issues. For example, what do you think should be the evangelical church's role in society? This stays away from deep personal disclosure, but yet gets you talking, relating, and getting to know each other in significant ways. Talk about a book you are both reading, your interests, and your hobbies. Talk about what's happening in your life, what you did last week, what your family is doing. Now. Stay away from "future talk", such as your highly personal hopes and dreams, or "past talk", like your greatest sins and regrets.

Emotional and physical intimacy should not be established yet. First Thessalonians 4:3-7 shows that it is dishonest to treat another person in a way that is to be reserved for one's spouse. The person you are dealing with is someone's wife or husband, and perhaps not yours. You would want to shake the hand of their spouse on their wedding day and know before God that you did nothing to hurt them, or to take what properly belongs only to a spouse. This is not only for their benefit, but also for the witness of the church (other believers as well as the watching world) and for the glory of God.

Now is the time to start drawing lines of accountability. And don't just be accountable to others in your age/peer group; they may be going through the exact same struggles you are, and thus limited in the degree of wisdom they can impart. Sadly, many young people act and live as if young people know everything, but this is nothing more than self-centeredness, naiveté, and arrogance. So find some older, married folk that you can trust. Secondly, biblical accountability is **you** seeking out people to be involved in your life. They are doing you a favor. **You** need to be the one setting the pattern of initiation to get them involved in your life. I say this because too many people think that accountability means someone else taking the initiative to follow up with them and otherwise chase them around. This seldom works because the one holding you accountable cannot read your mind, therefore he or she does not know all the questions to be asking you. Worse, because of our pride, we tend to hide our times of temptation and sin. So unless you decide from the outset of the relationship that you will pursue them, you might very well find yourself hiding your true struggles. Here are some practical suggestions. If it is geographically possible, invite your parents out to eat with you. Find older godly couples that you can get to know. Offer to help them out in their yard in exchange for some time with them. Commit that you will share how you are doing in specific areas with specific frequency (e.g. "Pastor Joe, I'd like to tell you each week how Lisa and I are avoiding sexual temptation"). One area in which you will particularly need accountability at this time is in how fast the relationship is moving. Frequently, couples start off way too fast, and this is especially problematic when the couple is young and unsure in what they are looking for in a spouse, and are not particularly ready to marry.

Another danger at this stage is that some parents start becoming "matchmakers" the instant their son or daughter gets involved. This is not helpful. Parents, you don't want to overly smash or squelch the interests of your children in this phase, nor do you want to needlessly accelerate the relationship just because you think the two make a "cute couple". In many courtship circles, there are parents who exhibit excessive control, either negatively (pushing the couple away from marriage) or positively (pushing the couple towards marriage).

3. Later Stages of a Romantic Relationship

Guys, again the brunt of the responsibility and initiation falls to you. Every day you stay in the relationship you are communicating to the woman that you are moving closer towards marriage than away from marriage. If, as you've been getting to know this person, you think it likely that you will want to propose, you need to tell her that you are getting more serious. It will become important for you to start discussing certain issues. Conversely, if either party does not think (s)he will be able to marry the other, the sooner the relationship is terminated the better it will be for all involved. Don't delay ending a relationship you know is doomed for fear of hurting the other person's feelings! This is itself hurtful and dishonoring.

An increasing degree of one-on-one time becomes appropriate. Note that this can frequently take the form of going on walks, or talking in coffee shops, restaurants, or malls. There is no need for this to take place late at night alone in your private apartment, however convenient it may be. Even if you don't give in to sexual temptation, it can give the appearance of evil, and it is unnecessary. Why put yourself in harm's way? Late at night you are far more likely to either fall into sexual temptation or simply be unable to have an intelligent conversation. Now is not the time to turn your brain off. You want to be alert and awake, asking good questions. Also, just because you are spending more one-on-one time together does not mean you should diminish the time you spend with mutual friends and older couples who provide individual or joint mentoring.

The discussion of deeper spiritual issues also becomes appropriate. Now is the time for couples to share more details regarding their testimonies, practical theological issues, goals, hopes, and dreams. There should be a commonality of goals and life-visions, and to the extent that there isn't, is there a willingness to make sacrifices? This may not sound politically correct, but a woman generally gives up more, in that God calls her to come alongside her husband and to help him in his calling. Is she willing to do this? What sort of nonnegotiables might she have? Must she stay in Sydney where she grew up, while he feels called to church-plant in Kazakhstan? Must she live within a few hours of her parents? A wise man will not want a miserable woman as his wife. Child-raising and other potentially emotionally charged issues should also be discussed. Practically, where might you live? What sort of work will you do? How is food to be put on the table? Will she work? When will you have children?

Please note that certain kinds of praying together, in private, can still breed excessive intimacy. A brief prayer of thanks before a meal or a prayer for the health of a cousin might be fine. But it is still too soon to be confessing sin together, praying about deep heart longings and struggles, asking for guidance on major life decisions, or spending prolonged periods together as a couple in worship. Each person is trying to pursue God at this time, and prayer together tends to communicate that you are making decisions together – as a couple. But you aren't; that's what engaged and married folk do.

Brother/sister displays of affection are not unlawful but may not be wise. There is a need to give consideration to whoever is more emotionally or sexually vulnerable. A man's sexual arousal generally occurs far earlier than a woman's, but a man can cause a woman to stumble in her thought life by frequent hugs or whispers of "sweet nothings". Beware of the relationship becoming a "drug", turning inward and becoming an end in itself. Remember that the relationship is to be marriage-directed, and even then the possible marriage is to be pointed towards the supremacy and glory of God, not itself.

I mentioned one role of the involvement of older couples at the early stages of a relationship was to help couples not to move too fast too soon. Now, at this later stage, godly mentors can help ensure that you are discussing the sort of topics you need to be discussing prior to engagement. And they can help keep you accountable with regard to physical and emotional purity. One practical measure is to have a clearly defined boundary with regard to physical purity, and then to regularly talk to the older couple(s) about how you are doing at maintaining that boundary. The accountability should also include asking the premarital couple questions like: "What kind of time frame are we talking about here? Where is this going?" Oftentimes, these questions need to be directed at the man. It is wise to not rush things, but many guys unnecessarily delay a decision due to fear of commitment. They wait too long to start asking themselves questions they should have been asking a long time ago.

Another reason why either might delay is the natural question, "How do I know there won't be someone better around the corner?" This question is common in our modern, individualistic age. After all, one can always get a new job in another town and meet other potential spouses there. Yet all choices involve limitations. The inability to make a choice is the undoing of many. The question should not be "Might there be someone better for me?" but rather, "Does this seem like the person God has brought into my life to marry?" Refer to Chapter 2 for my discussion on the idealistic notions people have regarding marriage and how it often contributes to the delay of marriage. Such idealism nowadays extends to the choice of a mate. We live in a youth-glorifying, physical-attraction-idolizing culture. If we compare our relationships to those in the movies, none of us measure up. But the movie world is make-believe, and the frequency of divorce in the lives of the "rich and famous" shows how illusory the chase for a "perfect" spouse can be. And if you think about it, most happily married folk are just regular people who chose to be committed and to learn every day how to love each other (in spite of those few extra pounds, or ever-multiplying wrinkles and gray hairs).

4. Leaving and Cleaving

So we come to the last stages of the relationship process. David Powlison and John Yenchko have written a helpful booklet entitled "Pre-Engagement: 5 Questions to Ask Yourselves"[5] in which they walk through numerous considerations regarding leaving one's parents and single years and cleaving to a spouse.

In leaving, each should be willing to leave their families emotionally and financially, and to leave behind the social and career aspects of their single lives. The emotional leaving is often harder for women. Yet failure to do this leads to problems, the woman who insists that all their vacations be taken with her parents; the woman who "goes home to her mother" – by phone or by physical visit – at the first sign of difficulty; the man who stops by his mother's house every day before going home to his wife; and the man who won't defend his wife against the criticism

5. David Powlison and John Yenchko, *"Pre-Engagement: 5 Questions to Ask Yourselves"*, Presbyterian and Reformed Publishing, 2000.

of either set of parents. Secondly, couples should be willing to break financially from their parents. Questions like these should be asked: Are you ready to care for yourselves and pay your own way, even if that means having a lower standard of living? For a young couple raised in a fairly affluent home, this decrease can be substantial. Thirdly, couples should be willing to leave socially: Is the man willing to break from going out with the guys three nights a week? A married woman likewise cannot make her best friends the source of all her emotional and spiritual satisfaction. Lastly, couples should make sure they are ready to break from career-oriented living, and make their spouse more important than optional career ambitions.

With regard to cleaving, couples should make an effort to see if they are aligned with one another on matters of the Christian faith that will impact their life together. Amos 3:3 asks the question, "Do two walk together, unless they have agreed to meet?" The idea of "walk together" here implies a level of agreement as to the destination and route. There are theological matters – like how one views the Scriptures, the doctrines associated with God's sovereignty and human responsibility, and baptism – that will influence how a couple raises a family, and how they would respond to any significant suffering that God may ordain (e.g. the death of a child). It is far better to be in agreement *in advance* on a theology that can sustain husband and wife, father and mother, in such times.

Along the same lines, discussing general expectations for a life together is wise. Where might the couple live? Near the biological families of one or both couples, or elsewhere? Might the family move from time to time? Will having children be a welcome event, and if so, when? Immediately after marriage, or will some form of birth control be used for a period of time? How often might parents be visited? How might holidays be spent? Cleaving also means that the marriage relationship becomes the top priority, after the relationship with God. All decisions about career, time, money, family, etc. are now made together, with the good of the marriage and the spouse set before the good of self. One should go into this, to the extent possible, with eyes wide open.

Discussion Questions:

1. Why is being part of a Christian community so important to the process of finding a spouse?

2. What are some of the dangers of exploring romantic relationships before you're ready (too young, no job, etc.) to marry?

3. Do you agree that it should always be the man who initiates the relationship? What are some of the reasons the author uses to support this? As a woman, have you been tempted to, or have you actually initiated the advancement of a romantic relationship?

4. Do you have any mentors or close friends that can hold you accountable? If you are not in a romantic relationship now, is there an older person or couple whom you trust? How about your parents?

5. What will be the most difficult aspects for you when it comes to leaving or cleaving?

6. As you look back over the whole book, what are some of the dangers or struggles you most readily identify with?

Other References

1. *The Mark of a Man*, Elisabeth Elliot, Ravell, 1981.
2. Resources for Changing Lives, *Marriage: Whose Dream?*, Paul David Tripp, P&R Publishing, 1999.
3. *Five Paths to the Love of Your Life*, Alex Chediak (with Jeramy Clark, Lauren Winner, Rick Holland, Doug Wilson, and Jonathan Lindvall), NavPress, 2005.
4. Pastor Rick Holland of Grace Community Church in Sun Valley, CA gave an excellent series on Relationships in 1999, all of which can be found (MP3 format) online: http://www.crossroadsministry.net/crossroads/mp3.asp?dlyear=1999.

Conclusion

Second to the commitment to follow the Lord Jesus Christ, who you will marry is one of the most important decisions – perhaps the most important – you will make. How you go about the process will reveal the extent to which Jesus is the Lord of your life. Wherever you may go, God has a people, His church, with whom we are called to live in community – learning, exhorting, and encouraging. I trust this book has encouraged you either towards lifelong celibacy according to God's unique gifting or toward marriage within God's family to His glory.

Most of you will marry. Develop and maintain relationships with godly mentors that can be with you in the process. "House and wealth are inherited from fathers, but a prudent wife is from the LORD" (Prov. 19:14). Men, I close by challenging you to embrace all that God has for you as men. Pursue God above all else, and ask Him to help you in identifying and pursuing a prudent wife. Seek to take responsibility and initiative in ways that honor others, remembering that one who would be great must be the servant of all (Matt. 20:27). Women, I close by challenging you to cultivate and treasure your femininity. Don't trade it just to have a guy. "Charm is deceitful, and beauty is vain, but a woman who fears the LORD is to be praised" (Prov. 31:30). And chastity with discretion gives you a sense of mystery that increases your value in the eyes of men. Remember that men value that which requires their pursuit. Seek your satisfaction and identity in God alone. Pray for a godly husband. Keep your eye out for and make yourself available to godly men without chasing them. Nurture, affirm, and receive strength from the right kind of men.

Remember that the Bible exhorts us to treat one another as brothers and sisters in Christ. Every Christian is your brother or sister, except that one who is your husband or wife. In seeking to identify that person, do not take what is not yours: honor brother and sister by not selfishly using them to gratify yourself emotionally or physically. It is emotionally misleading to date someone just to have companionship, when the possibility of marriage is nowhere in your thinking. It is likewise selfish and hurtful to seek to be physically intimate with someone outside of marriage. In God's economy, this never comes without consequences.

But oh, the grace that God extends to needy sinners who turn to Him in genuine faith and repentance! "From of old no one has heard or perceived by the ear, no eye has seen a God besides you, who acts for those who wait for him" (Is. 64:4). Did you hear what that verse is saying? **God** actually works **for** those who wait for Him. There is forgiveness and power for right living in Him. He loves to show Himself strong for those who humbly submit themselves to His lordship and treasure Him above all else. So no matter where you've been yesterday, seek Him for your tomorrow.

FAQs

1. What about dating/marrying non-Christians? After all, don't some people have happy family environments even though one of their parents may not have been a Christian? And likewise, don't some have negative experiences in Christian relationships?

The Bible is clear that marrying non-Christians is always sinful. Second Corinthians 6:14 gives the clearest support for this:

"Do not be unequally yoked with unbelievers. For what partnership has righteousness with lawlessness? Or what fellowship has light with darkness?"

The implied answer to both these questions is "none". In other words, Christians (who have been made righteous because of Christ) cannot have any true fellowship (i.e. partnership) with non-Christians (who do not submit themselves to God's law, and are therefore described by the term "lawlessness"). Elsewhere, Paul speaks of non-Christians (those who live according to the flesh, and who thus set their minds on the things of the flesh) as "hostile to God" and unable to submit to God's law (Rom. 8:5-8). To marry a non-Christian is to marry a potential spiritual enemy – and that for life!

If you would not marry a non-Christian, there can be no reason to date one. You are less likely to win them to Christ, as your example of disobedience will speak louder than any gospel words you may share. If they do come to embrace Christ it will be by the mercy of God in spite of your disobedience.

Yes, because of God's graciousness, many people have happy family environments even though one (or both) of their parents may not have been a Christian. In many of these cases, one parent becomes a believer after marriage, and then must live the remainder of life unable to share their best Friend with their spouse. Likewise, the fact that some Christian relationships go south does not make the romantic pursuit of a non-Christian appropriate.

2. What about masturbation?

Some Christians have incorrectly advocated the position that masturbation doesn't fall into the category of fornication because it is an individual act. Likewise, Christians who do masturbate placate their conscience with the notion that the Bible nowhere directly addresses masturbation. But this doesn't make sense because (for one) the thought patterns that accompany masturbation are generally unlawful lusts (Matt. 5:28). Even if one is thinking about their spouse, masturbation draws one into recreating the sex act alone and for purely selfish reasons. Yet God did not intend for sexual satisfaction to occur either alone or for purely selfish reasons. Rather, God intended sex to be a celebration of a lifelong covenant between a man and a woman. The sex act, not surprisingly, draws a man and woman out of themselves, and the happiness experienced by it depends in large measure on satisfying the other person. How much better to save sexuality for this context! "Let marriage be held in honor among all, and let the marriage bed be undefiled, for God will judge the sexually immoral and adulterous" (Heb. 13:4).

3. What about pornography?

In the United States alone, the annual revenue of the pornography industry is $12 billion. About

12 per cent of this comes from Internet pornography revenue. 12 per cent of all websites are pornographic. 25 per cent of daily search engine requests are related to pornography. Forty million American adults regularly visit pornographic websites.[1]

In many ways, pornography is the glaring (yet unspoken) problem in the Western church these days. It is a huge problem in and out of the church, and may be more common among professing Christians who, knowing God's standards, are perhaps less likely to commit adultery or fornication, but somehow feel less guilty indulging in pornography.

Pornography is clearly sinful, and ought to be fought with a two-pronged attack: negatively and positively. Negatively, to the extent humanly possible, all opportunities that create provision for the stimulation of lust should be avoided. Indulging in pornography always occurs *after* one has already succumbed to lustful patterns of thought – so the battle must first be won at the thought level. Spending less time alone, on the Internet (there are excellent pornography filters available), and in front of the television are generally helpful measures. Christians should likewise not tolerate sexual immorality in the movies they watch. This

1. These statistics are according to the Christian Science Monitor, August 25, 2005, "Churches confront 'Elephant in the Pews'", by Jane Lampman.

can be accomplished by either not watching certain films or by an adroit use of a remote control; each Christian should know himself and his weaknesses. Above all, a Christian should maintain a scripturally informed clear conscience. Often Christians emphasize the benefits of accountability partners – and they can be quite helpful, if one is honest and transparent with them. But at an even deeper level, a Christian's conscience is an almost sure judge of private failures (the ones considered too small to bring up with an accountability partner).[2] And private failures are what blossom into pornography usage and gross sin. So keeping a clean conscience is crucially important. Positively, cultivate your interest for the God-ordained, God-blessed pleasures of life. Take a walk on a sunny morning and look at the trees. Enjoy physical exercise and sports. Get enough rest. Nurture healthy ways to deal with stress or solitude. Develop friendships with both men and women so that you have strong emotional connections and don't feel so alone. Grow in your enjoyment of God by means of private and corporate worship. Finally, if unmarried, follow Chapters 5 and 6 in becoming and finding a great spouse – make it a priority in both your prayers and your activities.

2. One's conscience can be misinformed. But even here to go against conscience is neither safe nor right, as Martin Luther famously declared before the Diet of Worms (Rom. 14:23).

On this area, I'd also highly recommend two resources. Joshua Harris's *Not Even a Hint* (Multnomah, 2003) and *Sex and the Supremacy of Christ* (edited by John Piper and Justin Taylor, Crossway, 2005).

4. Are homosexual desires ever normal?

The nature-nurture question – the degree to which homosexual desires are transmitted genetically or biologically versus the result of purely voluntary choices – is beyond the scope of this book. No doubt, it is a very important issue in our day, and one in which Christians need to both lovingly and boldly proclaim God's truth. In short, I maintain that even if science were to prove that biology was one of a number of factors that give someone a propensity to homosexual activity, both homosexual desires and activity are always sinful. There is no contradiction; our bodies have been impacted by the Fall and all sinful expression is voluntary and, on some level, enjoyable and hence preferred. Yet God's grace extends to all sinners (and homosexuals are no different in this respect than liars, thieves, and gossipers).

For an excellent and more complete treatment of this topic, I would refer the reader to *Homosexuality: Speaking the Truth in Love*, by Edward T. Welch, Presbyterian and Reformed Publishing, 2000.

5. How far can a couple go sexually before marriage?

This is the wrong place to start for a variety of reasons. As I discussed in Chapters 5 and 6, men and women should be trying to determine (thoroughly, wisely, and largely objectively) whether to marry one another during their courtship. Since by God's design, physical/sexual intimacy bonds two individuals profoundly, thoughts (and feelings) become jumbled if affection is communicated physically prior to marriage. God intended such behavior to be foreplay to sex, and hence only to be experienced as part of the sex act itself. Consequently, both sexual intercourse and the foreplay that is meant to lead to sexual intercourse belong in marriage.

First Timothy 5:2 contains Paul's instructions to Timothy that he treat "older women like mothers, younger women like sisters, in all purity". All women a man relates to are either sisters/mothers in Christ, or a wife. Clearly, sexual intimacy and foreplay should be reserved for the latter. And the same would apply for women towards men.

The argument is sometimes made that hand-holding or walking arm-in-arm is meant to convey brotherly/sisterly affection. The standards I would encourage people to aim for are: don't do it, unless it is something you would do with your biological sibling. Don't do it if you'd be embarrassed by your behavior if Jesus Christ was physically present. Don't do it if you are aiming merely to please yourself (and are using your boyfriend/girlfriend to do so). Rather, communicate by your speech and by listening. Get to know each other more – in a local church context where God is treasured, and in which you both grow to increasingly love God more than life itself. That will make it a whole lot easier to commit and marry, and receive God's good gift of sex in His wise timing.

6. How do I know if this is THE person God wants me to marry?

You've been getting to know each other for the past year or two and everything seems to be going great. But you're just not sure you should settle down yet. I mean, what if someone better comes along? And how do you know if this person is actually THE person you are supposed to marry? What if someone else is God's will?

Questions like this haunt a surprisingly high number of people. You may have noticed that the Bible doesn't seem to give us the answer to this oh-so practical question of WHO??? But there is a little known Bible verse that addresses this very topic. Deuteronomy 29:29 goes like this: "The secret things belong to the Lord our

God, but the things that are revealed belong to us and to our children forever, that we may do all the words of this law." This verse says there are two categories of "things": "secret" things and "revealed" things. The revealed things are in the Bible – these include the principles we looked at in this book on how to become and find a godly partner. The secret things are just that: secret. They are not available to us. We're not supposed to try and find them. They're for God to know.

The same is true when it comes to thinking about God's will. In one sense, everything that happens is God's will, or else it wouldn't have happened. James 4:15 tells us we ought to say, *"If the Lord wills*, we will live and do this or that"* (emphasis mine). In other words, we may have plans to go to "such and such a town" (Jas. 4:13), but in reality we will only go there if it is God's will that we do. Otherwise, we won't. Yet there's another way that the Bible sometimes discusses God's will. First Thessalonians 4:3 says, "For this is the will of God, your sanctification: that you abstain from sexual immorality". So here the will of God is something we are TOLD to do. In James 4:15, we're to recognize that God's will may alter our plans. In 1 Thessalonians 4:3, we're to take heed to fulfill God's will ourselves.

How are we to understand this? The answer lies in Deuteronomy 29:29. In matters where God has revealed His will, we are to obey Him. In matters where God has not revealed His will, we're to trust Him. So in which category is finding a marriage partner? Tricky question. The answer is that it falls under both categories. God has revealed principles with regard to becoming and recognizing a godly partner. Yet God has not identified exactly which one of these potential partners we are to actually marry. So should this make us nervous? On the contrary, we should trust Him, recognizing that as we seek by His grace to live within His revealed will (following the principles in the Bible) *God will live out His will through us*. We can't miss His best for us. He wants us to have it more than we want it. As we walk down the aisle after making our wedding vows, we will know that he or she was God's will for us.

If this way of thinking is totally new for you, I'd like to recommend a book called *Decision Making and the Will of God* by Garry Friesen and J. Robin Maxson (Multnomah Publishers, 1999). It will radically free you from the anxiety associated with the false notion that we can and should discover God's secret will before it happens.

Other books
of interest
from
Christian Focus

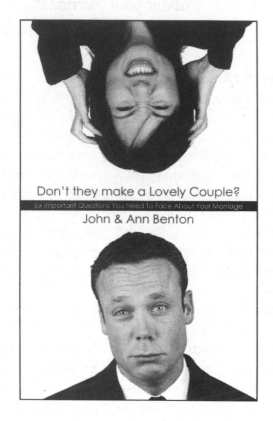

Don't they make a Lovely Couple?

Six Important Questions You Need To Face About Your Marriage

John & Ann Benton

Don't they make a Lovely Couple?

*Six important Questions you need to
Face about your Marriage*

Ann and John Benton

Only half of today's marriages stick – why is that?

The social revolution has made marriage fairer and unacceptable behaviour more 'frowned upon' so shouldn't our marriages be healthier and more long-lasting?

Why is it that an institution that forms the basis of society is in crisis? And what can we do to improve things?

Here are 6 questions to ask yourselves if you are preparing for, or are already part of, a marriage. This book won't make you feel guilty and suggest impossible solutions (we've all read THOSE sort of books before!). It'll make you realise what you can do and suggest a plan to implement it.

Is your marriage important? – Show that it is!

John and Ann Benton have developed and run practical Marriage orienting and enrichment seminars to the benefit of numerous couples (and couples to be). John is a church minister, author and magazine editor, Ann is also the author of the best-selling *'Aren't they lovely when they are Asleep?'* ISBN 1-85792-876-8 - an introductory book on parenting.

ISBN 1-84550-046-6

JOHN A. HUFFMAN, JR

the family

HOW TO BUILD AN AUTHENTIC, LOVING HOME

you want

The Family you Want

How to Establish an Authentic, Loving home

John A. Huffman

Whilst we all have a deep longing to be part of an ideal family, imperfect people make imperfect ones – it's a simple fact of life. Should we, as some in our post-modern society suggest, just give up?

If that thought depresses you then take heart and let John Huffman help you to achieve the best family you can. It won't be perfect but it will be better.

"With wisdom and winsomeness John has give us a book that can strengthen families and grow trust and love. I heartily recommend this book."

Jill Briscoe

"I highly recommend it... His approach is thoughtful, his style clear... this book is authentic."

Leighton Ford

"This most significant book carefully and clearly addresses the needs of the nuclear and extended family."

Ted Engstrom

"...here is healing medicine for all who care about the family"

Harold Myra, Christianity Today

John Huffman is the senior minister of St. Andrews Presbyterian Church in Newport Beach, California

ISBN 1-85792-933-0

A DEVOTIONAL FOR
COMPETITIVE PEOPLE

A SPORTING
GUIDE TO
ETERNITY

STEVE CONNOR

A Sporting Guide to Eternity

A Devotional for Competitive People

Steve Connor

You want to be on the winning team don't you?

"This book's for me! ...a valuable guide in your life and sports career."
Brian Irvine, Scottish International Footballer

"We all need guidance...this is a book of encouragement and devotion that will feed you with words of God, motivating you towards God's blessings."
Christian Okoye, NFL All Pro

"A great resource! ...for seeker to mature believer, on the spiritual compass."
Ron Frank, Fellowship of Christian Athletes

"I recommend it to everyone who wants to connect love of sport with a life of faith!"
Jerry Root, Wheaton College

Divided into topics which will be relevant to us all (such as anxiety, beauty, dealing with competition and prayer) this is a devotional for sportspeople – whether active or just armchair experts. Steve Connor shows how the message of Christianity can have a transforming effect on the life of sports-minded men and woman of every discipline.

Steve coached at Western Washington University, was an NAIA All American at Azusa Pacific University and had a short and un-illustrious NFL career with the Chicago Bears and Los Angeles (now St. Louis) Rams.
ISBN 1-85792-746-X

The Diamond Marriage

Have Ultimate Purpose in Your Marriage

Simon Vibert

THE
DIAMOND
MARRIAGE

HAVE ULTIMATE PURPOSE
IN YOUR MARRIAGE

GOD

HUSBAND — WIFE

THE
WORLD

SIMON VIBERT

The Diamond Marriage

Have ultimate purpose in your marriage

Simon Vibert

Few books on marriage provide satisfying answers. Why? Because of the focus. Mostly it's on 'me', sometimes it's on 'us' but rarely does it stretch beyond that.

This book is different! The emphasis goes beyond the husband and wife relationship and asks the questions 'Why has God gone to such great lengths to create marriage as we know it?' and 'what is its *purpose*?'

Packed with insight, wisdom, and wit, Vibert helps us to re-assess our views, provides new light on the same-sex marriage debate, and restore marriage to its rightful status – for us and before God.

"Here is a monumental work of love and energy, from one of the most effective Christian ministers today."

Richard Bewes OBE

"...sensitive, challenging, and born out of a clear biblical understanding of the subject matter."

Paul Gardner, Archdeacon of Exeter

"What a helpful, engaging, and God honoring book! Knowing it will help marriages at any stage."

Joel C. Hunter, Senior Pastor,
Northland, A Church Distributed

ISBN 1-84550-076-8

Christian Focus Publications
publishes books for all ages

Our mission statement –

STAYING FAITHFUL

In dependence upon God we seek to help make His infallible Word, the Bible, relevant. Our aim is to ensure that the Lord Jesus Christ is presented as the only hope to obtain forgiveness of sin, live a useful life and look forward to heaven with Him.

REACHING OUT

Christ's last command requires us to reach out to our world with His gospel. We seek to help fulfill that by publishing books that point people towards Jesus and help them develop a Christ-like maturity. We aim to equip all levels of readers for life, work, ministry and mission.

Books in our adult range are published in three imprints.

Christian Focus contains popular works including biographies, commentaries, basic doctrine and Christian living. Our children's books are also published in this imprint.

Mentor focuses on books written at a level suitable for Bible College and seminary students, pastors, and other serious readers. The imprint includes commentaries, doctrinal studies, examination of current issues and church history.

Christian Heritage contains classic writings from the past.

Christian Focus Publications, Ltd
Geanies House, Fearn,
Ross-shire, IV20 1TW, Scotland, United Kingdom
info@christianfocus.com
www.christianfocus.com